Tales of the Tempests

The Hurricanes of Kauai

Sheila Heathcote Arthur

ϟϟϟϟϟ

A Primitive Graffiti Book

Library of Congress Cataloging-in-Publication Data

Arthur, Sheila Heathcote, 1953 -
Tales of the Tempests

(A Primitive Graffiti book)
Bibliography:
      1. Hurricanes   2. Hurricane Warning System 3. Hurricane
      Preparedness
ISBN 0-9713413-0-3

Cover art by Lynwood Hume
Cover design and layout Sheila Arthur

This book is dedicated to the memory of my father, who taught me to be an adventurer; to my mother, who taught me to be creative; and to the people of Kauai, who taught me the real meaning of 'ohana.

Ino-ino mai nei luna
(Wild scud the clouds)

I ka hao a ka makani
(Hurled by the tempest)

He makani ahai-lono
(A tale-bearing wind)

Lohe ka luna i Pelekane
(That gossips afar)

From **Voices on the Wind: Polynesian Myths and Chants**, by
Kathrine Luomala, Bishop Museum Press, 1986.

Table of Contents

Acknowledgments

There are numerous people who were instrumental in the creation of this book. I'd first like to thank my husband, Michael, who encouraged me to persevere and not give up.

Hans Rosendal provided innumerable documents, maps, graphics, and references in addition to his expertise as a lead forecaster for the National Weather Service Honolulu office. Rosendal tracked Iniki firsthand from his workplace.

Keith Robinson was the person who actually got me started on this book. While I was conducting interviews solely about Hurricane Iniki, Keith told his harrowing story of being onboard the *Lehua* during Iwa. As I interviewed other residents, I found that many Kauaians had experienced more than one hurricane and that there were lessons to be learned from all of these collective experiences.

In the reference section at the end of this book, I have listed all the kind and generous people who took time out of their busy schedules to be interviewed. Without their stories this book would not have been possible. A loving "mahalo" goes out to all of those individuals for sharing their experience, strength and hope in the face of disaster.

Some of their stories evoked tears, and for that I am sorry. Other stories were told with a touch of humor, and a sincere appreciation of the wrath of a hurricane. Some of the people interviewed are no longer with us. May their memory live on in the pages of this book.

Aloha to Rick Rogers, who inspired me with his book on shipwrecks and to Georgia Mossman for the tips on publishing. And a special thanks to Sue Dixon who taught me the ropes of newspaper reporting, and Donna Stewart at H & S Publishing. Also a big thanks to Dr. Dudley, whose book on tsunamis guided and inspired me.

Foreword

The year 2002 marks the 100th anniversary of the Garden Island when most of the *Tales of the Tempests* on Kauai are chronicled.

Not for anything is Sheila Heathcote Arthur's timely message a warning and a prediction.

Writing on this, the 9th anniversary of Iniki, and in the dreadful shadow of the "Pearl Harbor of the 21st Century"' it is difficult to imagine a more cataclysmic upheaval in the light of a major shift in international politics: world climate patterns which could unleash catastrophic storms, predicted not only by the author, but by U.S. meteorologists as well.

In this well-researched and crafted chronicle, the lessons of hurricanes are clear: Emergency systems function on electrical power and when this fails, the whole system becomes inoperable (page 94). Public safety is at risk. Road conditions falter when utility poles collapse and telephones are no longer available. Radio and television stations are without power to broadcast updated bulletins to tourists, who are bewildered and oblivious as to what to do or where to go for shelter. Adequate temporary housing has been in short supply. The list is endless and quite disturbing in view of evacuation of our coastal areas in the event of a "super typhoon" or major tsunami, which would have far-reaching consequences for our island way of life.

Next time, don't ask whether there will be another hurricane. Ask, instead "When?" Preparedness is the ongoing message of this prophetic crusade as we turn the corner into our 21st century.

Dr. John Lydgate, President
The Kauai Historical Society

September 2001

Introduction

Ask most Hawaiian Islanders about Kauai's predisposition to intense weather and the majority will agree that Kauai seems to get the most rain, the worst floods and the only hurricanes. Since 1957, the island has been pummeled by hurricanes on four separate occasions.

Could hurricanes, along with other natural elements, simply be a natural part of the island's life cycle? The elements are credited with chiseling out Waimea Canyon and sharpening the breathtaking Na Pali coastline's silhouette. Rainfall and subsequent erosion have evoked landslides and carved out thousand-foot gullies where waterfalls plummet to sea level. Although storms and high winds have uprooted trees and flattened crops, winds and ocean currents have also brought plants, insects and other wildlife to the island.

Kauai is the most isolated of the four largest Hawaiian Islands, separated from its closest, heavily populated neighbor, Oahu, by a 60-mile channel. Kauai is also the oldest, the wettest, and the most eroded of the eight major islands. More than 5 million years ago, lava erupted out of the sea, and layer upon layer gradually formed Kauai's highest peaks, which may have reached 8,000 feet.

Over millions of years, past and future, rainfall and erosion slowly dismantle Kauai's fluted palis and gaping canyons, as the island drifts farther and farther away from its creator — the volcanic hot spot in the ocean floor over which the Big Island now rests. Riding on the Pacific Tectonic Plate, Kauai is gliding to the northwest at a rate of approximately 3.5 inches per year. As wind and rain continue to batter the island, Kauai will eventually become flat and resemble the atolls and sea mounts of the northwestern Hawaiian Archipelago.

The elements have shaped Kauai both physically and historically. Wind and ocean currents have affected settlement, exploration and even politics on Kauai, and have had some profound effects on those that came, or tried to come, to the island.

While the prevailing direction of the trade winds and currents generally opposed the direction of Polynesian migration to Hawaii, these skilled navigators were still able to reach the islands. The earliest dated settlements occurred around 300 A.D. on Oahu, Molokai and Hawaii Island, while Kauai was not inhabited by Polynesians until around 700 A.D. Archaeological evidence, such as the stone dressing of Waimea Valley's Menehune Ditch and the occurrence of ring or stirrup poi pounders — archaeological features unique to Kauai — may have occurred for one of two reasons. Kauai may have been settled by a group of different Polynesian voyagers than those who settled on other islands, or islanders may have retained older methods of tool making and stone dressing because of Kauai's isolation.

Kauai's relative isolation may not only have been geographically predisposed. Perhaps powerful currents and hurricane-force winds were more prevalent around Kauai, causing the island to be settled later than other islands. Surely, strong winds and currents would prevent Kauai settlers from leaving the island easily and may have protected Kauai from early invasion. No records, other than artifacts, exist from pre-contact times to confirm or disprove this theory; however, post-contact historical accounts show that quirky winds and currents plagued both explorers and marauders.

Kauai hosted the arrival of the first Westerners to Hawaii, when Captain James Cook and his crew of British sailors anchored near Waimea in 1778. After sailing from the Society Islands and briefly stopping on Christmas Island, Cook continued his northward journey and sighted land to the northeast. Wind and currents, however, prevented Cook from making landfall on this island, believed to be Oahu. But the following day, January 19, 1778, he took advantage of the winds and currents and reached the southeast coast of Kauai. Might hurricane winds follow a similar track?

Kauai was the only island to escape being physically conquered by King Kamehameha I. Following his conquest of Oahu in 1796, Kamehameha I assembled a huge fleet to attack Kauai. According to Western observers, there were between 1,200 and 1,500 canoes that would transport some 10,000 warriors, many armed with muskets, to Kauai's shores. In the middle of the 60-mile wide Kaieie Channel between Kauai and Oahu, the fleet encountered sudden high winds that capsized some of the advance canoes. Canoes that came to the rescue were also swamped. The strong currents of the channel wrought further havoc on the fleet as more canoes overturned or were sunk. Kamehameha I was forced to order the remainder of his fleet to return to Oahu. We can surmise, but cannot prove, that the winds encountered by Kamehameha's fleet in the Kaieie Channel were of hurricane force.

Regardless of whether or not hurricanes are a natural part of Kauai's environment, the manner in which island residents cope with severe weather is unique, and it may be more significant to Kauai's future than any type of scientific speculation. Kauai's people, who represent a conglomerate of different cultures, religions and ethnic backgrounds, have qualities that are found in few other populations. They live in harmony with one another and with the island that is their home.

There are several reasons why local residents may be better equipped to cope with strong, destructive winds. Many ancient Hawaiians survived volcanic eruptions, earthquakes, violent storms, droughts, floods, and famine. Not only did they learn to cope in order to survive, the population flourished.

During the last half of the nineteenth century, immigrant workers from distant countries — Japan, Germany, Puerto Rico, China, Portugal, Spain, and the Philippines — poured into Kauai to fuel the sugar and other booming agricultural industries. Despite the low-wage, backbreaking work, the promise of a better life beckoned the newcomers and enticed them to persevere and prosper. Many of these newcomers were familiar with harsh conditions, including droughts, tsunamis and famine, in their homelands. When hurricanes struck Kauai after 1956, wiping out power, water and communication, the sons and daughters of these hardy immigrants rolled up their sleeves and, with few complaints, went about their business without the conveniences of modern life. Even mainlanders who settle on Kauai quickly adapt to the island lifestyle and customs. Many mainland transplants have chosen Kauai because of its untainted beauty and rustic atmosphere. Collectively, most island residents are committed to protecting Kauai's rural character, and they willingly join their neighbors to confront unexpected acts of nature.

Four essential ingredients contribute to this unique fellowship, which is apparent in both times of crisis and in times of peaceful prosperity. Closely knit communities, strong personal values, intimate family ties and deep religious beliefs are parts of the common bond that unites most of Kauai's residents. In times of crisis, an unwavering spirit of camaraderie prevails, enables the community to deal effectively with the disaster and facilitates post-hurricane recovery efforts.

The personal stories of hurricane survivors that appear in *Tales of the Tempests* emphasize Kauai's multicultural affability and show how island residents sublimate their experiences. The book also highlights the history of hurricanes in Hawaiian waters, provides information about hurricane formation and prediction and stresses the ongoing need for hurricane preparedness.

For whatever reason hurricanes track through Hawaiian waters, it is unlikely they will ever cease. Although scientific data is provided and theories abound, no solid conclusions have been drawn about Kauai's inclination to be a target for hurricanes. Indeed, current scientific thought is geared toward preparing islanders all over the state for the inevitability of the next hurricane.

More research about hurricanes is needed. Perhaps *Tales of the Tempests* will stimulate interest in further research — both social and scientific — by providing a personal orientation to the weather phenomenon called the hurricane.

Kalaheo, July 2001

Chapter One

The Winds of Change

Between the "discovery" of Hawaii at Waimea Bay, Kauai by Capt. James Cook in 1778 and the time of statehood in 1959, the island underwent significant change. Western diseases ravaged the native population, and missionaries brought Christianity, thwarting many traditional, cultural practices. Additionally, the success of Hawaii's first large-scale sugar plantation at Koloa summoned hordes of entrepreneurs and immigrants to the island.

While still a U.S. Territory and leading up to the first significant weather event in "modern" history, Kauai carried on her local, plantation lifestyle stoically without much interference from the outside world. This sleepy island, drenched in sunshine and basking in isolation, was slow to invite further change.

But — like taxes and death — factors started to come into play that would have a profound impact on Kauai's residents and its economy. As the economic picture in the rest of the territory took a drastic downturn, Kauai was not immune to the winds of change.

Like upright dominoes ready to fall at the slightest provocation, Kauai's economy was ripening, only to be devastated by violent weather systems.

Hawaii's social and economic profile started to slowly transform during the years that followed World War II. With less military activity in the state between 1945 and 1950, defense expenditures sharply dropped from $800 million to $147 million.

Coupled with costly labor strikes, the territory plunged into the worst depression ever experienced in history. Four

1

years were necessary for Hawaii to recover from this economic crisis, which had left one out of five people without a job.

In the 1950s, the sugar industry prospered, but the pineapple industry fought tough competition from growers in other parts of the world. Labor shortages and high labor costs led to increased mechanization in these industries, and agricultural employment dropped by 38 percent between 1950 and 1960. However, opportunities in other businesses began to surface, including an increasing number of jobs in manufacturing and government service.

Like the capricious economy, weather systems that threatened the islands caught the attention of those in charge. Robert Simpson and the staff of the Weather Bureau Forecast Office in Honolulu were the first team to officially recognize a hurricane in Hawaiian waters*.

The date was August 12, 1950, and the storm was named Hurricane Able, or "Hiki" in the Hawaiian language. Hiki traveled on a course to the northwest, 100 to 200 miles offshore, nearly paralleling the windward coasts of the Big Island, Maui, Molokai, Oahu and Kauai. Hiki's course was temporarily blocked north of Kauai by an intensifying high-pressure ridge to the west on August 17.

Aircraft reconnaissance pilots noted that the hurricane was slowly being forced to the southwest and reported 90 mph winds south of the storm's center. Residents of Kauai and Oahu were alerted to a possible loop track that could propel Hiki through the channel between the two islands. Hiki, however, resumed its westward course when the westerly blockage dissipated.

Hurricane Hiki caused little wind damage, with 68 mph gusts recorded at Kilauea Lighthouse. The greatest losses were attributed to property damage associated with the flood-

---

* Hawaiian waters consist of an area within a radius of 100 nautical miles of Honolulu, south of 30 degrees north latitude and east of 140 degrees longitude.

ing of the Waimea River. Although no structures were swept away, more than 200 Waimea Valley residents had to evacuate, and many of their homes sustained considerable water damage. Hundreds of acres of cane fields were blanketed by water from Hiki's heavy rainfall, and the Kekaha powerhouse was badly damaged by flooding.

If these weather events affected the political leaders of the time, they didn't show it. The Democrats were busy attacking the old Republican-influenced system of low taxes for wealthy land owners, and the stage was being set for a new era in Hawaii's history — namely the development boom.

A report prepared in 1957 by the Economic Development Committee of the Kauai Chamber of Commerce backed development. "It would be of interest to the entire island to foster developments that will increase Kauai's job opportunities and keep a potential labor force from leaving the island," the report stated. The island's population declined from 29,683 in 1950 to 27,922 by 1960, leading economists to believe that development projects — by providing many new jobs — would be Kauai's saving grace.

Some displaced agricultural workers left Kauai because they had specialized skills that were not easily transferred to other types of jobs, and employers were experiencing difficulty replacing retired workers because many young people left Kauai to seek opportunities elsewhere.

In 1953 Kauai became the recipient of a modern highway project, several new schools and substantial dock improvements at Nawiliwili Harbor.

In 1955, developers built Kauai's first shopping center in downtown Lihue. A boom in the visitor industry was anticipated, and construction of resort properties at Poipu, Kalapaki, Waipouli, and Hanalei Bay were underway. When the first official hurricane struck, Kauai teetered on an undulating tightrope between the old days of agriculture and the new world of urbanization.

Hurricane Nina was considered a "minimal" hurricane, however, it served as a clear warning of what the future could

3

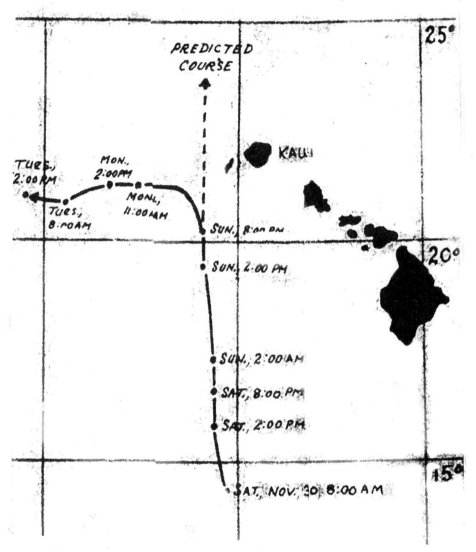

**Figure 1.1 Track of Hurricane Nina published in *The Garden Island*
Newspaper, Wednesday, December 4, 1957.**

bring once additional commercial and residential developments were in place.

§§§§§

Hurricane Nina

The summer of 1957 had been an unprecedented
hurricane season for Hawaii, with two threatening tropical
storms and three hurricanes that churned offshore waters but
avoided contact with land.

By late November, forecasters at the U.S. Weather
Bureau in Honolulu hoped that the remainder of the active
1957 hurricane season would remain quiet. It did not.

The Palmyra Island weather station received reports
of a tropical cyclone far south of Hawaii on November 29,
and immediately issued tropical storm warnings. The following morning, Saturday, November 30, the crew of a WB-50
took a turbulent ride into the eye of the storm to determine its
exact location and intensity (Figure 1.1).

The unwelcome visitor, christened "Nina" by weather
forecasters once it intruded upon Hawaiian waters, barreled
toward land.

Aircraft reconnaissance from the 57th Squadron at
Hickam Air Force Base determined that the storm's center
was 500 miles north of Palmyra and that it had intensified to
hurricane force. The next air reconnaissance flight reported
that Nina was southwest of the Big Island, at a reasonably
safe distance from land.

Remaining south of the island chain, Nina bypassed
Hawaii, Maui and Oahu, then slowed from 20 knots to six
knots while changing direction from north-northeast to north,
toward Kauai. In collaboration with radio, television stations
and the press, Weather Bureau forecasters warned the public.

By Sunday afternoon, December 1, as the late season hurricane spiraled toward land, forecasters predicted that

Figure 1.2 Front page of the *Honolulu Star Bulletin*, December 2, 1957.

would pass within 25 miles of Niihau. Shortly after nightfall, however, Nina again changed course, this time veering sharply to the west. Although Nina did not directly hit Kauai or Niihau — the eye remained 120 miles away from land — powerful,

arvin Brennecke's house at Poipu has a fatal attraction for both salt a

Figure 1. 3 Brennecke's Poipu home was photographed by Mike Fern and published in the December 4, 1957 issue of *The Garden Island* newspaper.

damaging winds, torrential rain, and high surf clouted both islands (Figure 1.2).

Nina's wind speeds recorded at Kilauea Point Lighthouse, even that far away from the eye, reached 92 mph.

Waves that reached heights of 35 feet at Poipu shattered the windows in the beachfront home of Mr. and Mrs. Douglas Baldwin. The chaotic surf blanketed their living room carpet with inches of dirty sand.

On the south end of Poipu Beach, boulders propelled by the raging surf, smashed windows and thundered into the Perin family's swimming pool. A few boulders exited on a receding wave, carrying away the home's front doors. Inundated and undermined by the storm surge, Akland Apartments became a brine-coated trap ready to collapse.

The once-elegant oceanfront home of Dr. Melvin Brennecke withered under the surf's onslaught. The house initially split in half, and then the waves pulverized the remains, rendering it a total loss (Figure 1.3).

Figure 1.4 Stairs (middle, right) to Poipu Bay inundated. Photo by Gordon Morse for *The Honolulu Advertiser*, December 3, 1957.

Nina gouged Poipu Harbor, leaving no trace of the breakwater or the cement dock, and ravaged the small boat club, destroying every boat that had been anchored there.

At the historic Koloa Landing, where tons of sugar cane and salted beef once departed for distant ports, the crashing surf regurgitated tons of rocks onto the small boat launching ramp, the dock and the old railroad right-of-way. South shore beaches were ravaged (Figure 1.4).

Along Maluhia Road, the tree-lined stretch that connects Koloa with Kaumualii Highway, uprooted eucalyptus trees and splintered branches littered the macadam like a gigantic, jumbled mass of pickup sticks.

In Hanapepe, Nina's howling winds ripped up trees and ransacked homes. A 50-year-old monkeypod tree — a Hanapepe community landmark — crashed into the home of Robert Fujimoto.

Fujimoto, who had been watching the tree throughout the storm, said, "It creaked and swayed so badly the ground shook." Fujimoto and his wife listened in terror as the tree

Figure 1.5 Kekaha Beach covers Kuamuali'i Highway following Hurricane Nina. Photo by Gordon Morse for *The Honolulu Advertiser*, December 3, 1957.

creaked and groaned, then toppled over. One of the tree's large branches pierced the corrugated iron roof over the living room, narrowly missing a few family members.

Saburo Akiyama, Robert Fujimoto's brother, shouted for help from his bedroom on the side of the house. The monkeypod's trunk crashed against the bedroom wall, pinning Akiyama to the bed. With a surge of superhuman strength, he pushed the wall far enough away to scramble to safety. More than a hundred neighbors later helped dislodge the tree from the house and clear away debris left by the storm.

At Kauai's westernmost community, Kekaha, a mile-long, scenic strip of Kaumualii Highway that previously bordered the ocean was buried in two feet of sand (Figure 1.5).

Many Kekaha residents were forced to evacuate their homes, and damage to buildings that housed the Kekaha Sugar Company was severe. At the outlying Mana Sugar Camp, near Polihale, the wind tore the roofs from four homes.

Conditions were not much better on the opposite side of the island, either. Under the brunt of the hurricane, the twin bridges connecting Wainiha and Haena with the rest of the north shore sagged dangerously, forcing officials to halt traffic.

On Wainiha Road, the Chandler family braced for the hurricane. Aunty Kapeka Chandler, who traces her family's genealogy back to pre-contact times when her early ancestors populated the verdant Wainiha Valley, recounted her Hurricane Nina experience with wide eyes and hands that gestured emphatically.

> "I had been living in a beach side home in Haena, but decided to move to Wainiha Valley, away from the coast, because of the number of tsunamis and storms that hit in the 1940s and 1950s. The first hurricane I remember was Nina in 1957. We just started building this house up here on Wainiha Powerhouse Road. The wind was strong but it really didn't do much damage, since we hadn't yet put up the walls. My husband was working for the McBryde Sugar Company at the time so we went to the plantation manager's home, up by the powerhouse at the end of the road.
>
> "I learned that the narrower the valley is, the worse the wind is. It was raining and flooding so much! You could hear the boulders rolling down this river. Boulders as big as this house! This hurricane, it changed the river completely. Where there were rapids, or where there were ponds, they all filled up. That stream (Kapeka points to a gently babbling Wainiha Stream running alongside her house) backed up into the power plant. We had about 32 inches of rain in this valley alone!"

On Kauai's eastern shore, in the Wailua district, the "Sleeping Giant" of Nounou Mountain appeared to be spouting like a whale. Rainwater that had collected at the summit began draining down the mountain's side, only to be captured by strong winds from the sea and sprayed spectacularly back over the mountain top.

At Nawiliwili Harbor, the breakwater was severely damaged, and three fishing sampans sank in Port Allen.

Rescue and recovery efforts commenced rapidly on Kauai as Nina swerved away from the island. Evacuation shelters opened at the Kekaha Armory and at schools in Waimea, Eleele, Kalaheo, Koloa, Lihue, Anahola, Kilauea, and Hanalei.

Kauai's plantation bosses joined Civil Defense officials in organizing an emergency communication network. Using the two-way radios in plantation vehicles, communication was assured when necessary and in the event that telephone communications failed.

Nina killed one Oahu man, electrocuted while working on a downed power line. Minor injuries were reported on Kauai, and Niihau took "quite a beating" according to a statement by the Robinson family which appeared in a December 2, 1957, *Honolulu Star-Bulletin* article.

Nina's high surf accounted for most of the $100,000 damage that occurred to structures along Kauai's south coast. Kauai was declared a disaster area by the Small Business Administration at the request of Governor William Quinn. Under the Small Business Administration's loan program, residents and businesses could later apply for low interest rate loans to rebuild.

§§§§§

By the late 1950s, mainland money started flowing into the territory for construction of new hotels and apartment buildings. Insurance firms, trust companies and large retailers such as Longs, Woolworth and Leeds, continued to bolster the state's economy.

Tourism was gaining momentum, particularly on Oahu, and it became necessary to accommodate larger numbers of tourists on the neighbor islands.

With the coming of statehood on August 21, 1959, mainland financial institutions and investors were poised to make even bigger investments in Hawaii. Prior to statehood, these investors were unsure of their legal status and what the territory's future may be.

The Big Five — Amfac, Castle and Cooke, Davies, Dillingham, and Alexander & Baldwin — expanded their businesses to the U.S. mainland and overseas, entered into real estate development in Hawaii and took stock control of the plantations they represented.

A residential real estate spurt in the late fifties altered Kauai's profile, particularly in beachside locations. The publisher of *The Garden Island* newspaper, C.J. Fern, reported some 1959 beachfront property values increased as much as 800 percent!

By 1959, only two years after Hurricane Nina, Kauai still retained some provincial characteristics. The island was, however, in transition. The visitor industry had not yet erupted as it would in future years, yet a number of small inns, starting with the opening of Kilauea's Polyglot Hotel, conducted a moderate amount of business.

Other hotels established in Kauai's early history included the Fairview Hotel in Lihue, the Ocean Hotel in Hanalei, the Beach Hotel in Kealia, and the Spouting Horn Hotel in Kuhio Park.

By 1959, construction of the largest resort to date, the Kauai Surf Hotel at Kalapaki Bay, commenced; plans for the Hanalei Plantation House Hotel hit the drawing board; and existing hotels on Kauai announced plans to expand their room capacities. Concurrent with the new tourist industry growth, hotel employment snowballed 234 percent between 1956 and 1962.

Only two weeks before Hawaii was granted statehood, Hurricane Dot ravaged the island of Kauai and laid waste to unfinished structures, crops and residences (Figure 1.6).

The newly developing island soon discovered how much more could be lost when a hurricane struck.

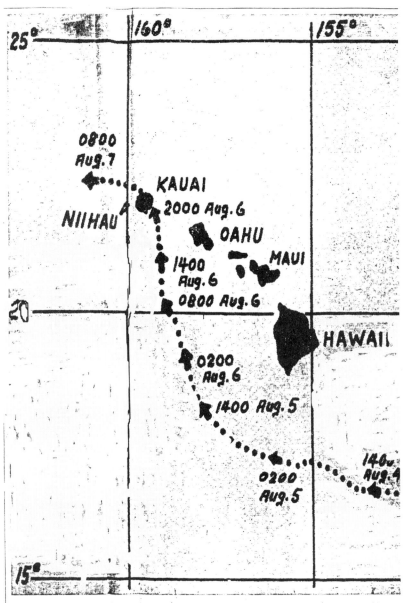

THE TRACK OF HURRICANE DOT—The above chart shows the track of Hurricane Dot as it approached the islands and passed over Kauai. The dates and times are the fixes as established by the Air Force and the Weather Bureau. The times shown are on a 24 hour clock taken every six hours at 2:00 and 8 threat of the hurricane became real a 12 hour basis.

Figure 1.6 Hurricane Dot's track according to Air Force and Weather Bureau fixes. Source: *The Garden Island* **newspaper, August 8, 1959.**

Hurricane Dot

On July 24, 1959, the S.S. Pacificus reported a tropical storm 1,000 miles west of Baja California, prompting the National Weather Service to issue a storm warning accompanied by the statement that "the accuracy of the (hurricane's) position was poor."

Over the next three days, the National Weather Service received no further ship reports about the storm and discontinued the advisories. But, on August 1, 1959, tropical storm Dot was officially detected when an unidentified ship reported encountering 60 knot surface winds on the periphery of Hawaiian waters.

On August 2, the S.S. Sonoma confirmed the previous account by reporting that it had passed through an area of low barometric pressure with 90 knot surface winds at 15.7 degrees north, 141.8 degrees west. Dot had developed into a full-blown hurricane.

Not until August 3 was Dot's position and intensity confirmed by aircraft reconnaissance. The hurricane's updated surface wind speed had increased to 140 knots (160 mph), and the large eye was between 35 and 40 miles in diameter.

Because it was the most intense storm in the modern history of the Central Pacific hurricane basin, the Air Force and the Weather Bureau closely monitored Hurricane Dot's track as it approached the islands. Reconnaissance pilots were measuring Dot's exact position, according to date and time with corresponding degrees of latitude and longitude, every six hours using a 24-hour clock.

On the morning of August 5, Hurricane Dot remained well away from the Big Island, then altered its path to a west-northwest track.

By 2 p.m. on Thursday, August 6, Dot's course again shifted, this time directly to the northwest, placing it on a collision course with Kauai. Although the best track placed the

First Photos Show Full Fury of Storm [Turn To Page A4]

REFERENCE

HURRRICANE ISOLATES KAUAI

NOW YOU SEE STEEPLE

NOW YOU DON'T

115-Mile Winds Rip Kauai; Power Lines Down, Rivers Up

Figure 1.7 *The Garden Island* newspaper, August 7, 1959.

eye west of Lihue, the total area of the storm was 962 square miles -- whereas the size of Kauai is only 553 square miles. Civil Defense officials expected heaviest destruction — mainly to the new and developing infrastructure — in Lihue and at Nawiliwili Harbor.

Preparing for the worst, the Hawaii National Guard, under Captain John M. English, established a transportation and radio network in Lihue.

By 4 p.m. the wind increased, Spouting Horn pumped out a sixty-foot plume, and 35-foot waves again battered Kauai's south shore. Radio Station KTOH lost its signal and went off the air at 6:15 p.m. Hurricane Dot made landfall around 8 p.m. slightly east of Makahuena Point, hammering the island with sustained winds of 81 mph and gusts up to 103 mph. Then Dot left Kauai near the Kilauea Lighthouse on the north shore (Figure 1.7).

Dot tore down power lines, demolished homes,

Figure 1.8 *Honolulu Advertiser* photo from August 8, 1959, photographer unknown.

Figure 1.9 This photo first appeared in *The Garden Island* newspaper on August 2, 1959 without a photo credit. It later appeared in the Home Insurance Company of Hawaii's brochuer dated April 4, 1960.

caused buildings to collapse, uprooted trees, clogged roadways with debris, flattened cane fields, and caused flooding
in low-lying areas (Figures 1.8 and 1.9).

Both the Hanapepe and Waimea Rivers flooded.
Waves washed across Kaumualii Highway in Kekaha and
on Kuhio Highway in front of the Coco Palms Resort.

During the evening of Dot's rampage, more than
1,000 people sought refuge in Kauai's designated hurricane
shelters, and the Red Cross reported that 203 dwellings, 6
farm structures and 689 other buildings had been destroyed.

At the Lihue Armory shelter, the staff battled the torrential rainfall, fighting to protect furnishings and important
files, while wading in nearly four inches of rainwater that had
accumulated on the Armory's floor.

According to news articles published in *The Honolulu Advertiser* and the *Garden Island* newspaper, Kauai residents had been given plenty of advanced warning by National
Weather Service forecasters who issued frequent bulletins
and updates to Kauai radio station KTOH.

Heeding the warnings, many of Kauai's businesses
closed early, allowing workers to return home to their families
and to secure their possessions.

§§§§§

Roger Dionne and his family were vacationing on
Kauai when Dot struck. Registered at the Coco Palms Hotel,
the Dionnes were on a day trip, enjoying the beautiful Garden
Island. Their excursion led the family to Kauai's increasingly
popular resort areas along the south shore. As luck would
have it, the Dionne family's sightseeing excursion included
an unexpected encounter with the forces of nature as Hurricane Dot drew near.

The Dionnes got more than just an eyeful while visit-
ing the Poipu area. "The waves were deafening," Roger
Dionne reported to *The Garden Island* newspaper. (According to hurricane trackers and National Weather Service meteorologists, Dot was predicted to come ashore in the area

PURNITURE MOVES AT KOKO PALMS

Figure 1.10   Moving furniture on the inland lake at Coco Palms Hotel after Hurricane Dot. Source: Home Insurance Company, Ltd. brochure, April 4, 1960.

---

between Makahuena Point and the rugged Mahaulepu coast-line).

Because the Coco Palms Hotel was so close to the ocean and in an area prone to flooding, special arrangements had to be made for their guests (Figure 1.10 and 1.11).

During the Dionnes' absence, Coco Palms evacuated its guests to the Wailua Ranch Hotel, where the electricity went out at about 5:30 p.m. Tourists huddling in the lobby and dining room of the Wailua Ranch Hotel watched in horror as the storm's increasing fury tore the roof off a neighboring house.

When they found out upon their return that Coco Palms had been evacuated, the Dionnes drove up Kuamoo Road to the Wailua Ranch Hotel. The place was packed and they discovered there wasn't enough bedding for those at the shelter, so they decided to try to get to St. Catherine's School on

ıi's Coco Palms Hotel was hard hit by the hurricane.
's how the hotel looked under four feet of water and ı

Figure 1.11　Coco Palms Hotel grounds four feet under water after Dot. Photo by Terry Luke, *Honolulu Star Bulletin,* August 8, 1959.

Kawaihau Road via the back roads.

At a particularly deep puddle that blocked the road, their car stalled. The Dionnes locked arms and tried to walk toward the school. The strength of the wind, however, forced them to find immediate shelter. They ran to the closest house, owned by Bill Brown, and pounded on the door. Brown ushered the Dionnes in, and they huddled with Brown and two other refugees in the center of the flooded main room. It was pitch black and the drenched ensemble listened to the walls and windows creaking under the wrath of the hurricane. Suddenly, the wind subsided from a "screeching violent thing" to practically nothing.

The Dionnes took advantage of the lull and again headed for St. Catherine's, this time successful in their attempt.

News reporter Betty Burleigh, also staying at St. Catherine's School, compared the shelter's atmosphere to a nightclub. "Directly across the hall, people were singing and playing the piano, and further down in one of the wings, a jazz combo was playing 'Little Grass Shack'. And, the catered dinner was a connoisseur's delight," Burleigh later reported.

She freshened her perfume and reached for the telephone to call her United Press office in Honolulu with an update on the hurricane and was surprised to find that the line was dead.

Toshichi Matsunaga's chicken coops at his commercial poultry farm in Lawai were in ruins, but most of the chickens escaped unharmed and were running helter-skelter around the property. The day after the hurricane, Matsunaga sold the chickens he could catch for 50 cents. Lawai was the hardest hit area on the island.

Keith Robinson, a descendent of the Sinclair family, who purchased the island of Niihau from King Kamehameha in 1863, was 18 years old and herding cattle on Niihau when Dot struck.

"It was oppressively hot and still the night before. I couldn't sleep; I was just sweltering. I came out of the family home on Niihau in the early morning to do some brandings. There were thick banks of clouds and a blood red sunrise, and it was still hot and oppressive. I was sleepy and I looked around and growled, 'We're going to have a hurricane today!'

"We got our branding done, and the wind started to rise. As I recall, it came in from almost due north, and started blowing slowly at first and gradually built up. When my dad and brother and the cowboys finished the branding in the middle of the hurricane, they drove the cattle back to their pasture and they all got covered thoroughly with dust. I mistakenly thought they didn't need me, so I rode a horse down to the beach to look at the ocean. It's lucky the horse's eyes weren't put out. The wind was driving the sand about ten feet high and there were terrible clouds. You couldn't put the back of your hand to the wind because the wind would just sandblast it. The wind swung around and then died around dark. My family said that during the cattle drive, a lot of big branches were breaking off the kiawe trees and this made the driving of the cattle hazardous, but there were no casualties among the men or the horses.

"On Kauai, when we came back a few days later, there were a few roofs blown off, but it wasn't a really terrible situation. In those days Kauai was relatively undeveloped and it had mainly old plantation housing. A lot of that old construction is pretty solid, so there was a lot less damage then than there would be with the kind of buildings you have nowadays."

Severe tree damage occurred in Waimea Canyon.

Figure 1.12 Kenzo Urabe surveys Kapaa store after Hurricane Dot. *Honolulu Star Bulletin,* August 8, 1959, photographer unknown.

Formed millions of years ago when Kauai's original shield volcano collapsed and created a deep fault, and further gouged by rainfall and drainage of the Waimea River, the canyon acted as a funnel for the hurricane's winds. Several hundred trees snapped or blew over, and thousands more were ruthlessly pruned.

§§§§§

Warmer than normal ocean temperatures in Hawaiian waters were cited as a probable cause for the storm by University of Hawaii geophysics professor Colin S. Ramage in an article that appeared in the *Honolulu Star Bulletin.*

Hurricanes had a tendency to slow and dissipate when reaching the cooler northern waters around the Hawaiian Islands. However, the El Niño, unknown at the time, had warmed Hawaiian waters and provided a suitable path that hurricanes could follow, gain energy, and grow. Hurricane

Figure 1.13 Lihue Plantation Company photo by Joe Shiramizu, September 14, 1959.

Dot followed a pattern — tracking toward the Hawaiian Islands from the south — set by her predecessor, Nina.

Called Kauai's "most disastrous storm" by the 1959 *Farm Plantation News*, Dot caused approximately $6 million (1959 dollars) in damages to Kauai alone (Figures 1.12 and 1.13).

Peripheral hurricane damage was evident on Hawaii Island due to the torrential rainfall. Some minor wave damage occurred at South Point and on the Kona Coast. On Oahu, local flooding and spot wind damage resulted from Hurricane Dot. While the highest recorded wind speed on the Waianae Coast was only 40 mph, damage to cars and loss of some roofs at Barbers Point indicated that some gusts may have exceeded 60 mph.

In some sections of Kauai, utilities were disrupted for a week, despite help from neighboring crews from Oahu. Edward E. Johnston, Hawaii's acting governor, requested disaster assistance from President Dwight Eisenhower, as damages far exceeded the minimum $1 million necessary to secure federal aid. The governor issued a Territorial Proclamation declaring a state of emergency, and President Eisenhower declared Kauai a federal disaster area.

Dot's costly damage to Kauai centered mainly on agricultural crops. Tree losses were especially severe on macadamia nut farms and resulted in heavy financial losses. Flooding cost the pineapple industry in excess of $200,000.

Kauai's agricultural industry continued to feel the economic impact of Hurricane Dot for several years. The sugar crop of 1959 would not be ready for harvest and sale until 1962, at which point final damages could be accurately assessed. According to a U.S. Department of Agriculture report, macadamia nut and lychee growers could not readily replace their lost trees, because new trees required a five-to-seven year growing period before they could bear fruit.

Following Hurricane Dot, the county of Kauai beefed up its emergency communications system by installing new transmitter receiver sets. These seven stationary and 14 portable sets would allow Civil Defense workers in outlying areas to communicate with headquarters in Lihue in the event of future power outages.

Hurricane Nina had remained comfortably offshore, and didn't have many long-term effects on the social and economic aspects of island life. Nina did cost money -- roughly $100,000 worth of storm damages on the relatively undeveloped south shore.

Two years and numerous development projects later, Hurricane Dot gave islanders a clearer picture of what happens when an island finds itself in the direct path of a violent weather system. Hurricane Dot marked a new era of damaging weather patterns that had at their mercy the newly constructed buildings and hotels that were supposed to assure Kauai's economic stability for the future.

The decline of agriculture also impacted Kauai's future. As development see-sawed with agriculture, and finally won out, millions of dollars tied up in new buildings and infrastructure stood to be lost.

In future years, it would be proven that crop recovery can occur more rapidly than reconstruction or the issuance of insurance settlement payments.

If only the people of Kauai and the state had known. The developing island of Kauai proved to be quite vulnerable to violent weather. Storms that Kauai residents surely experienced in the past were becoming money-chewing monsters because of development.

In the 1960s, increasing numbers of private residences, businesses and other developments flourished, but would later be subjected to even worse weather. The new boom of hotels, shopping centers and expanded infrastructure, such as highways, longer runways at the airport, bigger schools, and additional harbor improvements, would pose a new set of problems in the coming years.

Man-made structures, created without regard to the potential of hurricanes, would get the chance to compare strength and viability against the omnipotent forces of nature.

Legitimate developers would become painfully aware of the need for building codes to insure the safety and prevent the destruction of the new structures, while their unscrupulous colleagues would deliberately overlook this contingency.

§§§§§

Who ever imagined that Kauai's modern resorts, new commercial buildings and expanding private housing developments, that started in the 1950s and reached a pinnacle in the 1970s and 1980s, would fall victim to weather patterns that flirted with the island?

In subsequent years, people would believe that the increasingly brutal weather was to blame for all their losses and damages, rarely stopping to consider how vulnerable their modern world had become.

Figure 2.1   Satellite photo of a hurricane. Source: The National Weather Service.

Chapter Two

Anatomy of a Tempest

The hurricane is one of nature's most violent and turbulent events, a form of organized chaos produced by the ever-changing interaction between the sea and sky. At sea, the hurricane churns tropical waters as it removes and transports excess heat and moisture. Once in the atmosphere, this moisture turns to precipitation, and brings rainfall to crops that otherwise may have withered from drought. Upon striking land, however, the hurricane is one of the world's deadliest and most destructive storms.

Throughout history, hurricanes have caused billions of dollars worth of damage and have killed thousands of people, particularly when striking highly populated, low lying coastal areas of the world. The disaster potential of hurricanes is only likely to increase in the future. With the world's rapidly increasing coastal development and population, there are simply more targets for hurricanes to hit.

The term **hurricane** and **typhoon** are regionally specific names used to describe strong weather systems that have attained wind speeds of 74 mph and greater, generically specified as **tropical cyclones**. In the Caribbean Sea, the Gulf of Mexico, the north Atlantic Ocean, and the north Pacific Ocean east of the International Dateline, these storms are called hurricanes. Spanish explorers to the New World first encountered the word **hurricane** when they met up with natives who called their god of storms "Hurracan."

Archaeologists working in the steamy jungles of Central America discovered the first human record of a hurricane described in ancient Mayan hieroglyphs. Since the times of Columbus, hurricanes have been regularly encountered by ships traveling across the north Atlantic Ocean, as well as by settlers on Caribbean Islands and the eastern seaboard of the United States. In 1495, the small community of Isabella, founded by Columbus on the island of Hispaniola, became the first European settlement to be destroyed by a hurricane.

Typhoon, a mutation of the Chinese word for big wind, "te-fung," is the term used from the International Dateline to Asia. In the Indian Ocean basin, including the Bay of Bengal and the Arabian Sea, these destructive storms are simply called **cyclones**, a word derived from the Greek "kyklon", which means movement in a circular direction. Hurricane season in the eastern Pacific and in the Atlantic runs from the beginning of June until the end of November, while western Pacific typhoons can occur almost any time of the year. The reason why hurricane conditions vary depends on certain factors necessary for development, including a sea surface temperature of at least 80 degrees Farenheit, atmospheric instability that allows for the development of convective cloud formation and the appropriate latitude.

The **tropical cyclone** — generic for hurricane or typhoon — is a low-pressure system that arises over tropical or subtropical waters. An area within five degrees north or south of the equator is where the earth's rotation affects developing weather systems and gives them a cyclonic spin. In the northern hemisphere, tropical cyclones or hurricanes move in a counterclockwise direction, whereas in the southern hemisphere they rotate clockwise.

The tropical cyclone is marked by a warm core in which air temperatures in the center of the system are warmer than the surrounding environment. The tropical cyclone has definite cyclonic wind circulation and has developed organized **convection**, or thunderstorm, activity. Weather forecasters in the United States classify tropical cyclones in categories based on stage of development and peak sustained wind speeds.

In the early stages, humidity, warmth and weak trade winds fuel the development of a tropical cyclone. As the sun warms the tropical oceans during summer and autumn, sea surface temperatures rise to 80 degrees F (27C) or higher. This warming causes ocean water to evaporate, and the rising water vapor cools and condenses into rainfall and clouds. Convection, resulting from varying densities and temperatures in air-bone water droplets when they change back and forth from liquid into gas, allows for the release of huge amounts of latent heat into the atmosphere. Clouds form and amass and are propelled by rapid updrafts. When sufficient coolness has been achieved, the cloud contains enough ice and super-cooled water to separate and generate electrical charges. These towering cumulonimbus cloud formations, called thunderheads, produce thunderstorms that may group together, allowing conditions to become favorable for a **tropical disturbance** to develop.

The tropical disturbance continues to enlarge and develops a distinct, organized cluster of thunderstorms. If the disturbance maintains its identity for more than 24 hours and develops wind speeds up to 38 miles per hour, it becomes a **tropical depression**. As the system gains strength and size, it soon becomes a **tropical storm**, characterized by sustained winds ranging from 39 to 73 mph. The next stage is the fully developed tropical cyclone or hurricane, distinguished by wind speeds sustained at 74 mph (64 knots) and higher.

The fully developed tropical cyclone consists of a central, circular area of light and variable winds called the **eye** that can range in diameter from four to 40 miles. As the eye passes over land, taking anywhere from minutes to an hour, winds drop to near zero and the sky clears. Once the eye passes, however, hurricane strength winds — from the opposite direction — ensue.

Closely surrounding the eye is the eye wall or **core,** an area between five and ten miles wide, where the hurricane's most intense winds are concentrated. Called the **dangerous right semi-circle** (in the northern hemisphere) by mariners, the highest and most destructive winds are located near the core's center on the right side. Extending from the core outward are concentric bands of heavy rainfall that produce strong, gusty squalls that gradually diminish toward the outer edges. This outer region is the largest portion of the hurricane, and can extend over a distance 150 miles from the eye.

Extremely low pressure in the hurricane's eye sucks the ocean surface up by several feet, causing a rise in sea level called the **storm surge**. Exacerbated by the hurricane's advancing speed, wind direction and the contour of the ocean floor near land, the storm surge can develop into a wall of water 25 feet above average sea level.

Hurricanes are categorized according to their damage potential on a scale from one to five, called the Saffir-Simpson scale (Figure 2.2). Developed in 1971 by engineer Herbert Saffir and Dr. Roger Simpson of the U.S. Weather Bureau's Honolulu Forecast Office, the scale relates measured storm characteristics, such as peak winds and lowest pressure storm surge, to damage potential in terms of flooding, loss of vegetation, and structure performance. Tropical cyclones with sustained winds of more than twice normal hurricane intensity — 150 miles per hour or more — are called **super hurricanes** or **super typhoons**. Although several super typhoons occur annually in the western Pacific, super hurricanes are rare. In an average year, around 80 weather disturbances worldwide become tropical storms, and about half of these attain hurricane strength.

There are six areas where conditions encourage the genesis of hurricanes (Figure 2.3). These include the Atlantic basin (including the North Atlantic Ocean, the Gulf of Mexico and the Caribbean Sea) and the northeast Pacific basin (from Mexico to the International Dateline). Other areas are the northwest Pacific basin (from the dateline to Asia and including the South China Sea) and the north Indian basin (including the Bay of Bengal and the Arabian Sea). The final two areas of hurricane formation are the southwest Indian basin (from Africa to about 100 degrees east) and the Australian/

Category	Definition	Effects
One	Winds 74-95 mph	No real damage to building structures. Damage primarily to unanchored mobile homes, shrubbery, and trees. Also, some coastal road flooding and minor pier damage
Two	Winds 96-110 mph	Some roofing material, door, and window damage to buildings. Considerable damage to vegetation, mobile homes, and piers. Coastal and low-lying escape routes flood 2-4 hours before arrival of center. Small craft in unprotected anchorages break moorings.
Three	Winds 111-130 mph	Some structural damage to small residences and utility buildings with a minor amount of curtainwall failures. Mobile homes are destroyed. Flooding near the coast destroys smaller structures with larger structures damaged by floating debris. Terrain continuously lower than 5 feet ASL may be flooded inland 8 miles or more.
Four	Winds 131-155 mph	More extensive curtainwall failures with some complete roof structure failure on small residences. Major erosion of beach. Major damage to lower floors of structures near the shore. Terrain continuously lower than 10 feet ASL may be flooded requiring massive evacuation of residential areas inland as far as 6 miles.
Five	Winds greater than 155 mph	Complete roof failure on many residences and industrial buildings. Some complete building failures with small utility buildings blown over or away. Major damage to lower floors of all structures located less than 15 feet ASL and within 500 yards of the shoreline. Massive evacuation of residential areas on low ground within 5 to 10 miles of the shoreline may be required.

Figure 2.2 Saffir- Simpson Scale, courtesy of FEMA.

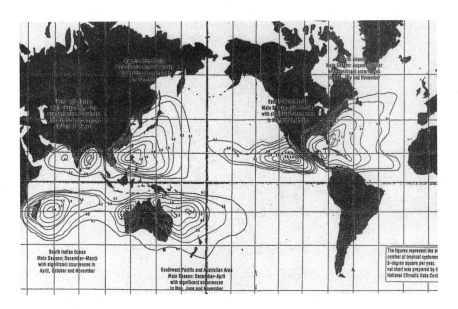

Figure 2.3   Hurricane Genesis regions. "The World of Tropical Cyclones". *Mariner's Weather Log,* Spring 1990.

Central Pacific tropical cyclone names

COLUMN 1		COLUMN 2		COLUMN 3		COLUMN 4	
Name	Pronunciation	Name	Pronunciation	Name	Pronunciation	Name	Pronunciation
AKONI	ah-KOH-nee	AKA	AH-kah	ALIKA	ah-LEE-kah	ANA	AH-nah
EMA	EH-mah	EKEKA	eh-KEH-kak	ELE	EH-leh	ELA	EH-lah
HANA	HAH-nah	HALI	HAH-lee	HUKO	HOO-koh	HALOLA	hah-LOH-lah
IO	EE-oo	INIKI	ee-NEE-kee	IOKE	ee-OH-keh	IUNE	ee-OO-neh
KELI	KEH-lee	KEONI	keh-OH-nee	KIKA	KEE-kah	KIMO	KEE-mo
LALA	LAH-lah	LI	LEE	LANA	LAH-na	LOKE	LOH-keh
MOKE	MOH-keh	MELE	MEH-leh	MAKA	MAH-kah	MALIA	mah-LEE-ah
NELE	NEH-leh	NONA	NOH-nah	NEKI	NEH-kee	NIALA	nee-AH-lah
OKA	OH-kah	OLIWA	oh-LEE-vah	OLEKA	oh-LEH-kah	OKO	OH-koh
PEKE	PEH-keh	PAKA	PAH-kah	PENI	PEH-nee	PALI	PAH-lee
ULEKI	oo-LEH-kee	UPANA	oo-PAH-nah	ULIA	oo-LEE-ah	ULIKA	oo-LEE-kah
WILA	VEE-lah	WENE	WEH-neh	WALI	WAH-lee	WALAKA	wah-LAH-kah

NOTE: Use Column 1 list of names until exhausted before going to Column 2, etc., All letters in the Hawaiian language are pronounced, including double or triple vowels.

Figure 2.4   Naming System for Central Pacific tropical cyclones. Courtesy of the National Weather Service.

Southwest Pacific basin (from 142 degrees east to 120 degrees west).

Once a tropical depression has been identified, weather forecasters assign it a number and letter according to its chronological order of formation in a given year.

Tropical storms receive names according to lists prepared by the World Meteorological Organization. Each year, a set of alphabetical names is assigned to the Atlantic Ocean and consists of common American first names. Another list, assigned to the Central North Pacific consists of first names in the Hawaiian language (Figure 2.4). Initially, hurricanes were given the name of the Saint's Day on which they struck, then in the 1950s, the phonetic alphabet — Able, Baker, Charlie — provided hurricane appellations. Once a major hurricane has struck land, its name will be removed from the lists and not used again.

Hurricane Patterns and Characteristics Around the Hawaiian Islands

Hurricanes that pose a threat to Hawaii can develop as far away as the coast of Africa or as close as the Line Islands — only 1,000 miles to Hawaii's south. The majority, however, originate in warm ocean waters along Mexico's west coast, in an area of favorable wind conditions and latitude. Most of the disturbances that move toward the northwest, however, tend to dissipate when reaching cooler north Pacific Ocean waters.

Disturbances that occur in the late fall months tend to move out to sea, slow down, wobble, then turn around and head back to Mexico and Baja, California, pummeling inland areas with flood-producing rain as far north as Arizona's Sonoran Desert. Some embryonic weather disturbances in the coastal ocean waters west of North Africa's Saharan region have developed into Atlantic hurricanes. Buffeted by the trade wind flow, these disturbances move out over the tropical Atlantic to encounter cooler water temperatures and dissipate or to develop into hurricanes that may continue across the Caribbean Sea.

Given optimum conditions, these African-born systems can even cross the isthmus of Central America and reach the warm coastal waters west of Mexico. In this prolific storm genesis area, the African-born system can strengthen and possibly continue west to threaten the Hawaiian Islands. The 1992 Hurricane Iniki was an example of this (Figure 2.5). Other disturbances that originated in Africa's western coastal waters have been traced through the Pacific and across the International Dateline, where they became deadly typhoons that threatened western Pacific islands and countries.

Other hurricanes that threaten Hawaii form near the equator in the Intertropical Convergence Zone, a common spawning area for tropical cyclones that straddles the Equator from about 3 to 9 degrees north. In this area of light and variable winds, evaporation and convection give rise to nearly continuous bands of heavy showers that can easily strengthen. Hurricane Dot, the 1959 tempest that brushed Kauai, formed here. Regardless of where a hurricane forms, there are conditions that can guide it to — or away from — land. These include topography, warm or cool seasonal water currents and wind patterns that can block, turn or dissolve a hurricane.

The elevation of islands of the Hawaiian Archipelago varies from a few feet to tens of thousands of feet, and the terrain encompasses nearly all of the world's climatic zones ranging from palm-lined beaches to snow-capped mountain summits. Pacific islands are classified as either high islands of substantial elevation or relatively flat landmasses called atolls.

The eight major Hawaiian Islands, with elevation ranges from 1,000 to 14,000 feet, are considered the archipelago's typical high islands and are the chain's youngest. To the north and west of the major islands lie the eroded and weathered remains of once-high Pacific Islands that have withered and flattened over millions of years to become atolls and, eventually, submerged seamounts.

While atolls have little effect on a hurricane's circulation and rainfall patterns and are easily engulfed by the storm

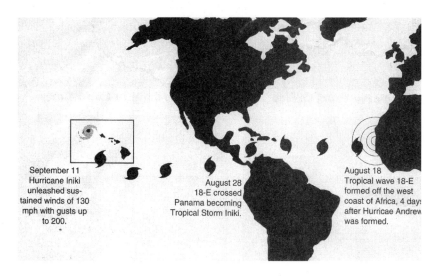

**Figure 2.5   Iniki originally developed off the coast of Africa.
Source "Iniki" 1992. H&S Publishing.**

surge, high Pacific islands may influence the path and the
severity of an approaching storm. The 14,000-foot volcanoes
of the Big Island, Mauna Loa and Mauna Kea, and Maui's
10,000 foot Haleakala are considered abnormally tall volcanoes. Some meteorologists believe that massive volcanoes
such as these deflect and disrupt hurricane winds and circulation patterns. These enormous mountains may also cause
the system to steer away from Maui and the Big Island, which
explains why smaller, lower elevation islands — like Oahu,
Kauai, Niihau, and others downstream from Hawaii and Maui
— seem to be less protected from damaging hurricane winds.

A phenomenon called wind shear can also impact the
path of a hurricane. When winds change direction, increase
in elevation and speed up rapidly, this significant variation, or
shear, can disrupt and blow away the cyclone's warm air and
prevent further storm development. Along with the prevailing
northeasterly trade winds, the Hawaiian Islands generally have
large vertical wind shears, which serve to diffuse heat and
moisture and, may cause hurricanes to break up. A lack of
shear is an important component in both the development

and growth of the hurricane. Hurricane winds on exposed mountain slopes and ridges of moderately high islands, Kauai included, are profoundly altered by the terrain and result in a wide range of localized wind speeds. When hurricane winds encounter terrain of varying heights and contour, consider-able air flow modification results. Winds decelerate when moving upslope and forcefully accelerate when hurling downslope. Mountain peaks and gaps reroute air flow, and create venturi effects, similar to raging river currents that funnel through narrow, land-flanked straits (Figure 2.6).

The El Niño

The Coriolis effect and the earth's rotation governs the predominant trade winds in the northern and southern hemispheres. Air resting above the steamy ocean waters of the equator begins to rise and flows away to the north and south. When this air reaches an area between 25 and 40 degrees latitude, it piles up and causes an area of high at-mospheric pressure. Some of the cooled air, which is denser and heavier than the warm air at the equator, descends from the high-pressure area and returns to the equator.

There it is swept by the Coriolis force to the right (clock-wise) in the northern hemisphere, which causes the north-east trade winds. The same thing happens in the southern hemisphere in the reverse, where airflow returning to the equa-tor rotates to the left (counterclockwise).

Trade winds play an important role in the development of immature tropical cyclones, especially where the El Niño is concerned. The El Niño Southern Oscillation (ENSO), a disruption of how the ocean normally reacts with the atmo-sphere, affects weather patterns around the world. Droughts occur half a world away in Southeast Africa, unusually cold weather envelops Greenland, and flood-producing rains pelt portions of South America and in southwestern U.S.

A Spanish term for the Christ child, the El Niño is an unusual warming of surface waters over a large portion of the tropical Pacific, and it occurs when trade winds in the central and western Pacific weaken. The El Niño — once thought to

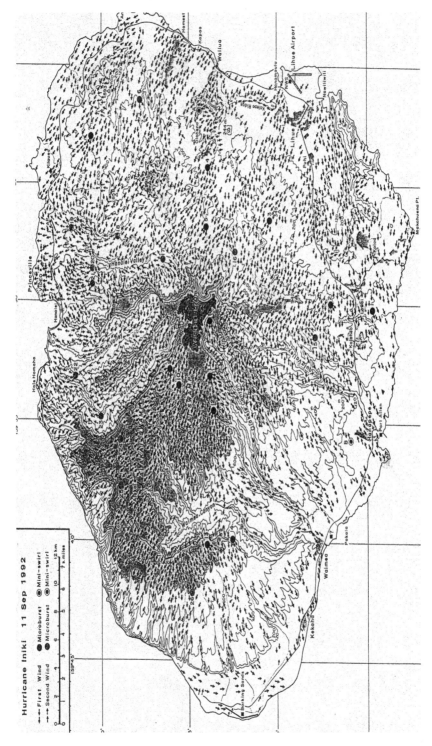

Figure 2.6   Accelerated wind speeds on Kauai during Hurricane Iniki. Courtesy of the National Weather Service.

flank only the coastal waters of Peru and Ecuador — has been shown to cover a vast part of the Pacific Ocean. Conversely, La Niña is the opposite, referring to a period of cold surface waters in the Pacific. The fluctuation between the cold and warm water periods, termed the Southern Oscillation, is the atmospheric response to the cycles of changes occurring in sea surface temperature.

Normally, trade winds cool the surface of the sea and blow from east to west across the Pacific. This warm surface water, roughly about eight degrees higher near Indonesia than the ocean along the coast of South America, triggers abundant rainfall in response to the evaporation of surface waters. Along coastal South America, nutrient-rich cold water from deep within the ocean circulates to the surface. Abundant with marine life, this cold water allows for only minimal evaporation of the ocean surface and results in relatively dry conditions for surrounding land areas.

During an El Niño, however, the faltering trades in the central and western Pacific Ocean cause equatorial ocean temperatures to rise from five to ten degrees, forcing the cold water along the South American coast to sink. Without the upwelling of cool surface waters along South America, sea surface temperatures rise (Figure 2.7). Rainfall follows the warm water eastward, causing floods in Peru, while normally warm-water areas with abundant rainfall, like Australia and Indonesia, experience severe drought. El Niño typically lasts 12 to 18 months and has a recurrence interval of approximately three to five years.

The Hawaiian Islands are particularly vulnerable to El Niño cycles that affect the neighboring Line Islands. During non-El Niño years, the atolls of the Line Island group may experience three or four successive years of minimal rainfall and abundant sunshine. In contrast, El Niño usually causes drought conditions in the Hawaiian Islands as winter rains decrease. During El Niño years, however, the Line Islands are buffeted by light westerly winds that allow tropical cyclone genesis to occur. Nina in 1957 and Iwa in 1982 are examples

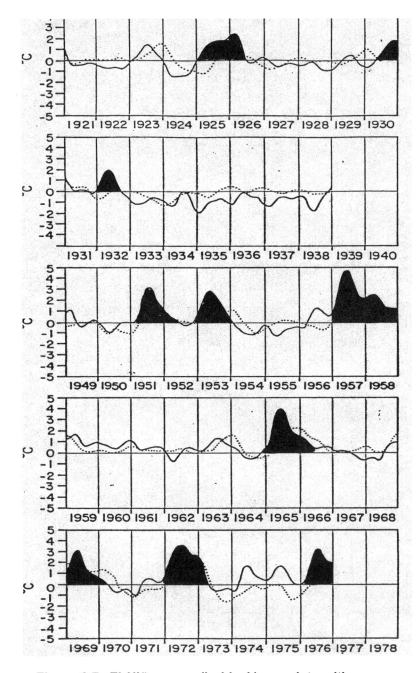

Figure 2.7 El Niño years (in black) correlate with warmer water temperatures. (The WWII years were classified information and not released). Courtesy Hans Rosendal, National Weather Service.

of hurricanes that formed in this region during periods of westerly equatorial winds. Both these late-season hurricanes formed in November near the equator, during an El Niño cycle.

By 1982, scientists were just beginning to understand the association of the El Niño to record numbers of tropical cyclones. Reported by the Hurricane Vulnerability Study post-Iwa, the peak number of hurricanes in 1957, 1972 and 1982 appeared to be related to the occurrence of very strong El Niño conditions during those years. The strongest El Niño cycle on record occurred during 1982 and 1983, shortly after the Mexican volcano El Chichon erupted and enveloped the earth in a stratospheric dust veil. Some scientists speculated that this eruption might have contributed to the increased ocean temperatures. Thick cloud layers of volcanic emissions may slow the trade winds and cause the ocean to become warmer due to the subsequent lack of cool breezes.

El Niño occurred again in 1991-1993, when hurricanes almost simultaneously assaulted south Florida, Guam and Hawaii. Similarly, the 1991-93 El Niño developed shortly after the very dusty eruption of Mount Pinatubo in the Philippines. Whether there is a direct relationship between the eruption of low latitude volcanoes and the onset of El Niño is still a hypothesis under scientific investigation. Pollutants and industrial emissions, as well as other factors that contribute to global warming or the greenhouse effect, have also been blamed.

ϛϛϛϛϛ

Chapter Three

The History of Hurricanes in Hawaiian Waters

From the early 16th century come the first records of the destructive nature of hurricanes. Christopher Columbus lost most of his fleet in 1495 in a Caribbean tempest. Columbus, however, was able to protect a subsequent fleet in 1502 stationed at Santo Domingo by predicting the arrival of a hurricane. This fleet had adequate time to find safe harbor and rode out the event with little damage because of Columbus's experience and knowledge.

Following the discovery of the barometer in 1643 by Torricelli, the German geographer Bernhard Varenius described hurricanes as great "whirlwinds" in his book, *Geographia Naturalis*. Between the mid-1600s and the mid-1800s, additional information about the nature of cyclones came from mariners' ship's logs.

Brilliant seamen and scientists in the early 1800s developed synoptic weather charts (invented by Professor H.W. Brandes) and showed counterclockwise cyclonic circulation patterns. Although the destructive power of these storms caused considerable damage on land and at sea, measuring accurate and gale-force wind speeds in the years from 1832 to 1949 had yet to be perfected.

The Beaufort Scale

The Beaufort Scale invented by Rear Admiral Sir Francis Beaufort provided visual guidelines to determine wind speeds before wind-measuring equipment existed. Beaufort devised

Code No.	Description	Pressure lbs per square foot	Wind Speed miles per hour	Wind Speed knots	Observable Effects on the Environment
0	Calm	0	less than 1	less than 1	Smoke will rise vertically.
1	Light Air	0.01	1-3	1-3	Rising smoke drifts, weather vane is inactive.
2	Light Breeze	0.02	4-7	4-6	Leaves rustle, can feel wind on your face, weather vane is inactive.
3	Gentle Breeze	0.28	8-12	7-10	Leaves and twigs move around. Light weight flags extend.
4	Moderate Breeze	0.67	13-18	11-16	Moves thin branches, raises dust and paper.
5	Fresh Breeze	1.31	19-24	17-21	Trees sway.
6	Strong Breeze	2.30	25-31	22-27	Large tree branches move, open wires (such as telegraph wires) begin to "whistle", umbrellas are difficult to keep under control.
7	Moderate Gale	3.60	32-38	28-33	Large trees begin to sway, noticeably difficult to walk.
8	Fresh Gale	5.40	39-46	34-40	Twigs and small branches are broken from trees, walking into the wind is very difficult.
9	Strong Gale	7.70	47-54	41-47	Slight damage occurs to buildings, shingles are blown off of roofs.
10	Whole Gale	10.50	55-63	48-55	Large trees are uprooted, building damage is considerable.
11	Storm	14.00	64-75	55-65	Extensive widespread damage. These typically occur only at sea, and rarely inland.
12	Hurricane	above 17	above 75	above 65	Extreme destruction.

Figure 3.1 The Beaufort Scale, invented by a British Naval Commander in 1805, has been updated and is still used today. Courtesy of Scott Trudell's Weather Page internet site.

this wind force scale in 1805 when he became the commander of the Woolwich, a 44-gun man-of-war.

The Beaufort Scale describes conditions ranging from Force 0 to Force 12, which provides a numeric wind speed "force" that is described in terms of the ship's characteristics under sail and the effect of the wind on the sea surface (Figure 3.1). The Beaufort scale has also been adapted for use on land.

By 1838 the Beaufort wind force scale had become mandatory for log entries in all ships of the Royal Navy.

The conversion from Beaufort's visual sea characteristics to a wind speed scale was facilitated by technology. In 1837, Samuel Morse demonstrated the first practical telegraph, and in 1846, T. R. Robinson invented the cup anemometer. Neither of these inventions would have saved Beaufort's scale, however, if it weren't for a catastrophe.

In 1854, the English and French were entrenched in fighting at Sevastopol. An intense, early winter storm on the morning of November 14, however, proved to be an even worse adversary. Both the English and French fleets suffered more damage from the storm than they had from even the most savage battle. In response to the losses, and with the hope that there might be some way to forecast future storms, the British Admiralty and the French Marine Corps jointly sponsored a weather network, the ancestor of the World Meteorological Organization, to provide storm warnings.

In 1912, the International Commission for Weather Telegraphy sought some conformity on velocity equivalents for the Beaufort scale. A uniform set of equivalents was accepted in 1926 and revised slightly in 1946. By 1955, wind velocities in knots replaced Beaufort numbers on weather maps.

From 1832 until 1949, according to Samuel L. Shaw's *A History of Tropical Cyclones in the Central North Pacific and the Hawaiian Islands* and other historical documents, roughly one significant cyclone grazed the Hawaiian Islands on an average of every four years (Figure 3.2).

According to Shaw, the earliest record of a tropical cyclone in the central north Pacific occurred in 1832 and appeared in a German Merchant Marine ship's log. Called the Deutsche Seewarte I cyclone, the tempest came within 350 miles of the Big Island's South Point.

In one of the first books about Hawaii, James J. Jarves, an ambassador to Washington, D.C. who represented King Kamehameha III, and an editor of the 1840 *Polynesian Newspaper*, recorded his observations about weather patterns in the islands. From the pages of *Scenes and Scenery in the Sandwich Islands and a Trip Through Central America 1837-1842*, Jarves reported:

> *"These islands are not subject to the hurricanes common to other tropical climates, though occasionally it blows sufficiently strong during the winter months, to prostrate the frail habitations of the natives, and do damage to the trees."*

An article in the *Pacific Commercial Advertiser* of October 10, 1868 may be the earliest documented newspaper report of hurricane activity to affect the Hawaiian Islands.

> *"DAMAGE ON KAUAI—By the schooner "Nellie," we learn that the wind which was here quite fresh until last Friday and Saturday 1-2 October, blew a heavy gale on Kauai. At Nawiliwili considerable damage was done to the cane fields. At Koloa the surf rolled in furiously, tore away the wharf, carried some twenty cords of wood to sea, and did other damage. At Hanapepe four houses were blown down, and at Waimea seven more were destroyed. A portion of the roof of the large church there was also blown off. A large number of trees were uprooted, while scores of coconut trees were broken*

off as if they had been pine stems."

A second article about the same storm, appeared in the *Hawaiian Gazette* of 14 October 1868, which was published in Honolulu by M. Raplee, the Director of the Government Press.

"THE STORM--The southerly wind and rainy weather that we had in Honolulu from September 19 to October 8, prevailed throughout the group. The rains have been copious and abundant, and most favorable for plantation crops.

"There was not any heavy and damaging wind except on Kauai, where, on Saturday, October 3, it blew almost a hurricane, chopping all around the compass. At Lihue about $5,000 dollars damage was sustained in the breaking down of the cane in the fields. The water flume of Mr. G. Wilcox was thrown down. At Koloa, the sea swept away the wharf and caused other damage. The fury of the gale seemed to culminate around Waimea, where several houses were thrown down, and the fine stone church building was extensively damaged. Two thirds of the northern wall of the building fell, racking and straining the roof frame and otherwise damaging the whole structure.

"In Honolulu on Thursday, October 1, the barometer stood at 30.05, wind N. E. moderate. It fell in the next twenty-four hours to 29.90, wind still N. E. but squally. On Saturday it chopped suddenly to the S. E. with heavy squalls and rain, and the barometer remained at 29.90 until the following Monday. The weather is still unsettled although the rains have abated."

In September 1870, the Deutsche Seewarte II cyclone

was tracked to a point about 50 miles below South Point. The *Pacific Commercial Advertiser* of September 24, 1870 reported an account of this event in its "Notes of the week" section:

> *"The equinoctial storm which old salts always look for about this time, appears to have burst on us in the shape of a heavy gale of wind, accompanied by rain squalls. Should the wind veer a point or two further south it will probably give us an abundance of rain, for the atmosphere is warm and damp."*

The Kohala cyclone of August 9, 1871, a strong cyclone that impacted both the Big Island and Maui was described in August 16 and 23 issues of the *Hawaiian Gazette*. The article included graphic accounts of the storm provided by Kohala Sugar Company plantation manager D.D. Baldwin and by a Kohala resident, the Reverend Bond. The Rev. Mr. Bond relates:

> *"About 150 houses were blown down, trees in ravines torn up like wisps of grass, cane stripped and torn, as never before and even the grass forced down and made to cleave to the earth."*

The Kohala Cyclone also affected Maui, according to the following mariner's report:

> *"On Wednesday last (August 9, 1871) the Island of Maui was visited by one of the most severe, if not the severest, storm that has been felt on any of these islands for many years. At Lahaina the storm, which appears to have been a most violent cyclone, commenced about ten o'clock and ranged for several*

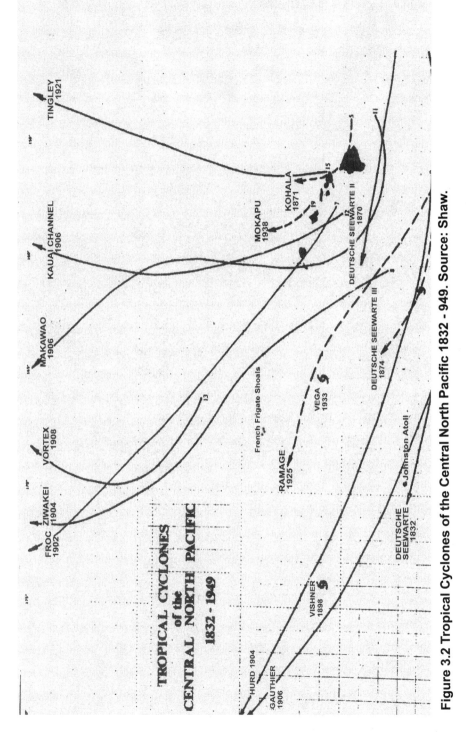

Figure 3.2 Tropical Cyclones of the Central North Pacific 1832 - 949. Source: Shaw.

47

In an article entitled, "The History of Waimea", which appeared in *Waimea, Island of Kauai 1778-1978*, a storm of hurricane proportions assaulted Waimea with disastrous results. The article notes:

"The historic Waimea Church had its roof blown off in a storm in 1885" (Figure 3.3).

The next major storm, tracked by the Reverend Louis Froc, Director of the Ziwakei Observatory, Shanghai, was called the Froc cyclone. The storm began about 40 miles southwest of Lanai on December 23 and on December 24, was located in the Kaulakahi Channel between Kauai and Niihau. It dissipated in the Bering Sea in early January 1903.

Between 1904 and 1906, Shaw noted five cyclones in the central north Pacific. The October 1906 Makawao cyclone was first recorded 120 miles southeast of Hilo and traveled to about 60 miles south of South Point. Also in the same year, the Kauai Channel cyclone churned between Kauai and Oahu from November 6-9, 1906.

In the years between 1910 and 1928, nearly 100 cyclones were reported to the U.S. Weather Bureau, many from information supplied by the Mexican meteorological service. The apparent increase in cyclonic activity paralleled the increase in ocean traffic and reporting of storms.

The Panama Canal opened in 1914, and following the Great Depression of 1921, came an increase in ocean commerce.

Ship reports during this era pinpointed the Vega cyclone of August 1923 at 450 miles south of Honolulu, and it caused wave damage and high seas on the southwest coast of Kauai.

Reported in the *Honolulu Advertiser* on August 2, 3, and 4, 1925, the Ramage cyclone caused considerable damage to the Big Island and Honolulu.

"Late in the afternoon of the 1st, an exceptionally

Figure 3.3. The Waimea Foreign Church following Iniki in 1992. This wasn't the first time the church lost its roof in a hurricane.

---

high tide accompanied by strong winds flooded the wharf warehouse at Honuapo on the Big Island. All beach houses there were flooded. The unusually high winds caused a long line of flumes at Hutchinson Plantation to collapse. Honolulu experienced record surf heights for this time of the year. Fort Kam was flooded, lawns were awash and damaged by huge breakers on the beaches at Diamond Head and Kahala; beach houses and properties 'on the other side' of the island were flooded and damaged."

On August 19, 1938, the *Honolulu Star-Bulletin* reported the Mokapu cyclone.

"Between midnight and 3 A.M. a gale tore over the island, reaching great proportions with a velocity of 60 miles an hour recorded at an American radio

station at Mokapu."

The *Honolulu Advertiser* in December 1957 published an article called "Old Timers Recall Bygone Storms." The article reported eight violent storms between 1904 and 1938 which are believed to have been winter storms and associated cold fronts instead of tropical cyclones. These are excerpts from the *Advertiser's* reports:

* On February 11, 1904, a storm struck the Hawaiian Islands that "made Waipio Valley on Hawaii look like the Mississippi River.

* On January 18, 1906, a storm was reported that "made the blow of 1904 look weak."

* On December 3, 1918, the wind "hit 52 miles an hour and cut off radio communication with the outside world." Honolulu incurred $.5 million in damage, according to the *Advertiser's* account.

* A quarter-million dollar loss on Oahu's North Shore, which included washed out railroad tracks, followed the storm of January 16, 1921.

* Two vicious hailstorms pelted Oahu on March 23, 1927, and February 27, 1935.

* Two separate storms that washed out Kalihi Valley in 1930 killed a total of nineteen people.

* Another storm on January 27, 1938 "tore out bridges all around the islands."

Three of the six most critical storms that approached the eight main Hawaiian Islands between 1832 and 1949 barreled toward Kauai and Niihau.

The Froc Cyclone skirted Kauai's southwestern shores, the Makawao Cyclone ran directly over Niihau and the Kauai Channel Cyclone rolled dead center between the islands of Kauai and Oahu.

It seems that hurricanes may have been an ever present threat to Kauai and the other islands, or that more were be-

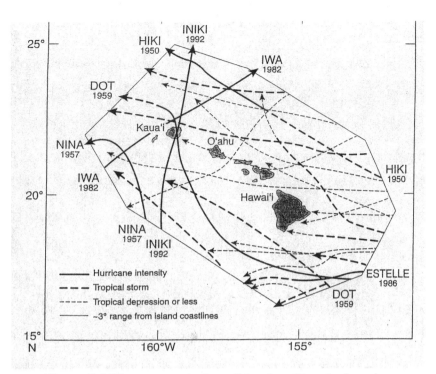

Figure 3.4 Diagram capturing all tracks of tropical cyclones passing nearby the islands between 1950 and 1992. Source: Schroeder

ing observed and reported (Figure 3.4).

An article that appeared in the *Honolulu Star Bulletin*, December 2, 1957, by Robert L. Johnson, claimed that Kauai's first major hurricane of the century was "the fourth hurricane this year to develop in waters where it has been said, up to now, hurricanes do not develop."

Chief Meteorologist Dean Perry at the Weather Bureau, Honolulu Airport, said in the same December 2, 1957 article:

> *"The British Admiralty Weather Glossary says hurricanes do not occur in the (central portion of the) eastern North Pacific. Up to this year I had no reason not to believe that."*

While historical documents and old newspaper accounts show that Hawaii has had many severe storms and gales, meteorologists of the 1950s were scientists on a new frontier. The new methods of identifying developing systems, tracking these systems through stages of intensity, and accurately measuring wind speeds to determine hurricane-strength storms would further prove the British Admiralty Weather Glossary wrong.

As far as the Hawaiians who navigated the vast Pacific to reach these volcanic specks of islands, dealing with tempests was just a normal part of being a voyager. They revered many winds, winds of different places and strengths, winds of various names and description.

In translations of ancient chants, such as *The Wind Gourd of Laomaomao* (Nakuina, 1990), hundreds of different winds from all parts of the Hawaiian Islands are recognized. Certain winds could be summoned from Laomaomao's calabash to do everything from sinking an enemy's canoe to luring enough fish to a certain fishing spot to feed a hungry village.

There is, however, not a specific word for the hurricane in the Hawaiian language.

"In my research of Hawaiian chants, literature and dictionaries, I have not been able to find a Hawaiian word for 'hurricane'," said Lilikala Kame'eleihiwa, Assistant Professor of Hawaiian Studies at the University of Hawaii at Manoa.

§§§§§

Chapter Four

The Calm Before the Storm

Between Hurricane Dot in 1959 and Hurricane Iwa in 1982, there was a period of relatively calm weather in the vicinity of the Hawaiian Islands. Economic activity during this period, however, was anything but calm. Hotels, high-rise apartment buildings and condominiums were popping up on Oahu and Maui faster than weeds take over an untended garden. Hawaii's sunny and mild weather, with a few exceptions, didn't intrude on island life and facilitated construction projects in the islands.

During this era, Hawaii reached its financial pinnacle when the economy experienced its largest gains in the state's history. On Kauai, it took a bit longer for development to get underway. Some political leaders and citizens--who watched with trepidation as Oahu and Maui residents welcomed or ignored their encroaching concrete jungles--rallied against rapid growth. On the other side were those who sought the same prosperity for Kauai that her sister islands were experiencing.

Those who were pro-development included some politicians, many businessmen and numerous Kauai residents who desperately needed jobs. While Hawaii's leaders were enjoying the flourishing economy, a few threatening weather systems came close enough to the major islands to be a menace. Weather events that could have served as a "heads up" for builders and those who regulated the building codes were, however, mostly ignored.

The sixties were a time of growth and change. Hawaii's burgeoning construction industry took advantage of major technological advances in urban and residential construction. Similarly, weather forecasters also took advantage of important new technology, developed during the space race between America and the Soviet Union, that aided them in tracking developing hurricanes.

The first meteorological satellite, Television Infrared Observation Satellite I (TIROS I), was launched from Cape Canaveral on April 1, 1960, and marked a new era of hurricane awareness and forecasting. Except for Hurricane Hiki, the pre-satellite detection of tropical cyclones in the central north Pacific* depended on ship reports and was mainly confined to areas in the vicinity of principal shipping routes.

According to Shaw, early weather satellite data suggested a far greater frequency of tropical cyclones in the vicinity of the Hawaiian Islands than had been previously observed by traditional meteorological data.

A comparison of the data provided by the early TIROS satellites and the conventional U.S. Weather Bureau's 1962 and 1963 monthly tropical storm summaries showed that only five of 22 tropical storms were detected by ships. Of the 22 tropical storms, six were located in the central north Pacific, and posed a potential threat to the state of Hawaii.

The Hawaiian Islands in the 1960s, particularly during the hurricane seasons of 1962, 1967 and 1968, witnessed a few tropical storms, depressions and hurricanes. While Hawaii had its fair share of bad weather in 1962, 24 destructive typhoons threatened the western Pacific, from the Malay Peninsula to the International Dateline, killing 1,700 people and causing more than $325,000,000 dollars in property damage.

Not until 1966 — one year after a significant El Niño cycle -- did a hurricane form in Hawaiian waters (Figure 4.1). Hurricane Connie's 86-knot wind speeds were the highest

*Pacific Ocean waters surrounding Hawaii north of the Equator from longitude 140 degrees west to the International Dateline.

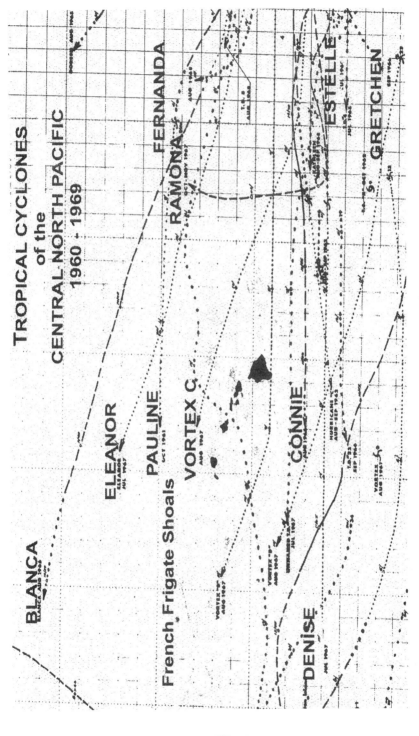

Figure 4.1. Tracks of tropical depressions, storms and hurricanes 1960 - 1969. Source: Shaw.

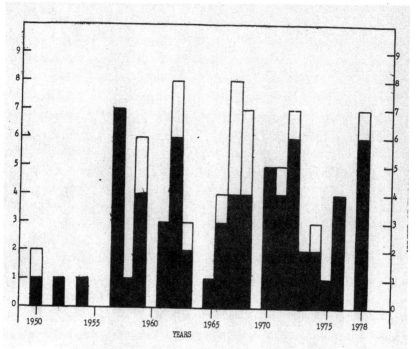

Annual distribution of the 85 tropical cyclones (open bars) and the 74 tropical storms and hurricanes (solid bars) that entered or formed in the Central North Pacific, 1950-1978.

Figure 4.2. Source: Shaw .

noted east of the International Dateline in 1966.

The following year, 1967, was touted as "the year that Diamond Head stayed green" by weather forecasters. Record-breaking amounts of heavy rainfall assaulted the main islands, hail was reported on Maui's Haleakala and at the summit of Mauna Kea on the Big Island, Oahu experienced several minor rock slides, and Kauai's Hanapepe, Wailua and Hanalei Rivers flooded. Also in 1967, tropical storm Sarah glided past the Hawaiian Islands, intensified to hurricane strength and crushed Wake Island with 116 knot winds. The remainder of the 1960s brought mostly fair weather and inactive hurricane seasons.

In 1970, significant hurricane activity occurred in central north Pacific and began with tropical Storm Maggie. Unusually heavy rainfall pelted the Big Island, resulting in local flooding, landslides, and crop damage. In 1971, tropical storm

Sarah brought strong winds and locally heavy rains over the entire state. Lanai Airport had to be closed, and five homes in Molokai's Hoolehua district were damaged. Gusts up to 66 mph were recorded at Kokee. Hurricane Denise, also in 1971, brought badly needed rainfall to the Hamakua district of the Big Island, while stranding motorists on flooded roadways in Kailua-Kona.

In 1972, seven tropical cyclones entered or formed in the central north Pacific, and 12 developed in the eastern North Pacific--slightly below the 1966-1972 annual average of 15. The 1972-73 El Niño cycles reached the intensity of previous El Niños that occurred in 1891, 1925, 1941, 1957-58, and 1965 (Figure 4.2). Maui reported beach erosion from high surf, and six inches of rain fell along the northeast coast due to Hurricane Diana's close approach of only 30 nautical miles north of Maui. Hurricane Fernanda, another 1972 storm that impacted Hawaii Island, caused a flash flood in Waipio Stream due to heavy rains in the Kohala Mountains. Hurricane Celeste passed 380 nautical miles below South Point, pounding the Puna, Kau and South Kona coasts of the Big Island with 15-foot surf. With maximum sustained winds of 120 knots, Hurricane Celeste later became one of the three most intense hurricanes on record in the central North Pacific. No hurricanes were reported in the central North Pacific in 1975.

Meteorologists examining other weather anomalies reasoned that cooler sea surface temperatures and a vertical shear resulting from a prevailing westerly upper atmospheric flow may have inhibited hurricane development. Hurricane Kate came within 300 nautical miles* of the Big Island on September 28, 1976, and forecasters issued a hurricane watch for that island. The watch was abandoned when Kate downgraded to a tropical storm the following day. Hurricane Kate generated surf up to 15 feet along the northern and eastern shores of Hawaii, Maui and Oahu, but no serious dam-

* One nautical mile is equal to 6,087.15 feet or 1.15 miles.

age was reported.

During the 1978 hurricane season, weather forecasters witnessed a record number of cyclones in the central North Pacific. Thirteen cyclones or their identifiable remains entered or formed in the area. Hurricane Fico was cited as one of the most intense hurricanes on record and traveled more than 5,000 nautical miles while maintaining hurricane intensity for 17 consecutive days. Gusty winds up to 50 knots belted all the Hawaiian Islands, and 30-foot surf reported by Big Island Civil Defense officials flooded coastal roads and caused significant damage to beach front homes. Unable to make headway against the 50 knot winds, six people aboard a 43 -foot sailboat near Hanalei had to be rescued by a Navy torpedo boat. Near Kauai's south shore the Lihue III, a 65-foot tugboat, ran aground near Kukuiula Harbor.

With maximum sustained winds of 120 knots, the final hurricane of the active 1978 season, Susan, also became one of the three most intense hurricanes on record, surpassed only by Hurricane Patsy's 150- knot maximum sustained winds in 1959.

As weather systems intensified near the end of the decade, development reached its pinnacle, and there was no way to turn back.

Like the rest of America during the 1960s and 1970s, the Hawaiian Islands experienced dramatic change, as the financial focus shifted from agriculture to a predominantly tourism-based economy. While there were surely opponents to rapid growth on Maui and Oahu, none were quite as vocal as those belonging to Kauai's strong "grass-roots" movement were. A political tug of war-between rich developers and citizen groups opposed to development--emerged before the billowing dust of the bulldozers could settle. Compromise was the name of the game, and a new crop of ecology-minded political leaders were able to put the dampers on some construction projects, but were unable to limit them all.

Former Kauai mayor, JoAnn Yukimura, was one political leader, in particular, who rallied for carefully controlled development. Yukimura attended Stanford University and the University of Washington Law School from 1967 to 1974, then returned to Kauai to practice law. Yukimura served on the Kauai County Council from 1977 to 1980 and ran unsuccessfully for mayor in 1980 and 1982.

"The joke in those days was that the state bird was the (construction) crane. Everywhere you looked on Oahu there were high rises going up. I became aware of the challenges and dangers of rapid growth issues when development was inundating Waikiki and Maui. Kauai too, was under pressure to grow rapidly. A grass-roots movement began when I was in college. By the mid- 1 9 70s, when I returned, a very active community had evolved."

During this time, major resorts were being planned for Princeville, Kilauea, Poipu, and Mahaulepu, and medium to large-sized residential projects were being proposed for Lihue, Wailua Homesteads and Kalaheo. Amfac, one of the largest landholders in Hawaii, sold large parcels of land, including the 1 1,000-acre Princeville Ranch in 1968 and the 60-acre parcel at Nukolii in 1973, along with prime commercial property in Lihue. In 1974 Congress allowed the Sugar Act to expire, and sugar prices began to decline by 1975. The year of 1977 became "the worst year ever in terms of (sugar) profitability." In 1980, however, Hawaii's sugar fetched the highest prices in history, due to poor sugar crops in other parts of the world. This sweet prosperity crashed again in 1981 with losses of about $100 million.

Hotel occupancy rates on Kauai had risen steadily, from 58 percent in 1970 to 80.6 percent in 1977. While Kauai's population had grown only seven percent during the decade of the 1960s, it increased at twice that rate between 1970 and 1977. A 14-acre parcel of land in Nawiliwili, which had multifamily zoning for many years until the owner sold it to a developer in 1974, became the site of the Banyan Harbor Resort condominiums constructed in 1977. JoAnn Yukimura describes the setting:

> "The Kilauea Agriculture Association was fighting a convention center complex in Kilauea, tenants in the Niumalu-Nawiliwili area were battling eviction, and the Ohana O Mahaulepu was contesting proposed development for Mahaulepu. What started as a ground swell in those early days turned into a tidal wave that broke on Nukolii in the mid-seventies. That parcel of land went back and forth between agricultural and resort zoning until 1982, when Hurricane Iwa disfigured Kauai's economy and landscape. With local people desperate for jobs, the developer won out and built the Kauai Hilton, which is now the Outrigger Hotel."

As the 1980s approached, Kauai's political leaders fueled the winds of change and developed ways to check the island's financial woes. One of those politicians, whose political career commenced in 1954, had already laid the groundwork for the large-scale development that was to be his legacy.

Tsuneto "Tony" Kunimura was born on April 12, 1923, the 11th child of Sadajiro Kunimura and his picture bride. Growing up in Koloa, Kunimura was part of a group of friends called the "Blackfoot Gang", named so because they were always covered with soot from the burning cane fields near their homes. Armed with a "cane field education" and a background as a meat cutter at Sueoka's store, Kunimura became a self-taught politician who embraced every challenge and opportunity he encountered, thus building a respected name for himself in Hawaii's political structure. Since childhood, Kunimura watched Kauai evolve from a semi-impoverished island dependent on agriculture, to its debut as an international, top-rate visitor destination.

Kunimura's colorful, 34-year political career began well before statehood. Disillusioned by labor laws that affected himself and other plantation workers, Kunimura ran for and was appointed to a position on the County Board of Supervisors. During his eight-year tenure, which began in 1954, Kunimura chaired the Finance Committee and began the first school bus service for Kauai's children. He also initiated legislation that acquired land for the development of Wilcox School and the War Memorial Convention Center.

While development was a hallmark of the Kunimura administration, he was also the man who introduced the 1959 Kauai county ordinance decreeing that, "No building shall be taller than the tallest coconut tree."

In 1962, Kunimura ran for, and was elected to, the State House of Representatives. He served as Finance Committee chairman and as the majority whip for the House of Representatives. During his 18 years on the State Finance Committee, Kunimura secured money for the development of Kauai's senior citizen's community centers, additional libraries, bigger schools, and improved roads. He was also instrumental in acquiring the land on which Kauai Community College now stands. In 1971, Kunimura urged his friend, Sam Wilcox, to ask Grove Farm to donate 200 acres of land in the Puhi area for the college, and Grove Farm complied.

While JoAnn Yukimura rallied the slow growth faction, Tony Kunimura helped to usher in the winds of change that soon would alter not only Kauai's profile, but also the very essence of the island's soul. Kunimura would soon have an ally named "Iwa".

ⰜⰜⰜⰜⰜ

Chapter Five

The Wild Frigate Bird -- Iwa

On Monday, November 22, 1982, the residents of Kauai--like most Americans--looked forward to the upcoming Thanksgiving holiday, set to fall on Thursday, November 26. Prior to November 22, the National Weather Service, via satellite imagery, calmly noted the presence of a tropical storm 600 miles south of the Hawaiian Islands. It was not until 5 p.m. on Monday, November 22, that Iwa picked up speed and became classified as a full-blown hurricane. Weather forecasters clenched their teeth as Iwa barreled north toward the fiftieth state.

Named for the great frigate bird, Iwa had some unusual characteristics. Iwa occurred outside the traditional hurricane season and, unlike most storms, came from the south instead of the east. Iwa formed in the central Pacific close to the equator, near the Line Islands, where Hurricane Nina had formed twenty-five years earlier. Additionally, Iwa's forward motion speed approaching Kauai was two to four times faster than the normal rate for hurricanes coming from the east.

The National Weather Service notified Civil Defense officials, who declared a hurricane watch for the islands of Kauai, Niihau and Oahu at 11 p.m. on Monday, November 22. Most of the early-to-bed, early-to-rise islanders were asleep when the hurricane watch was announced.

On Tuesday, November 23 at 8 a.m., Civil Defense officials upgraded the hurricane watch to a hurricane warning and radio stations quickly broadcast the warning. According to Kauai's Civil Defense Administrator, Sonny Gerardo, adequate shelters had not been established. Also, at the time of the hurricane warning's broadcast, most of

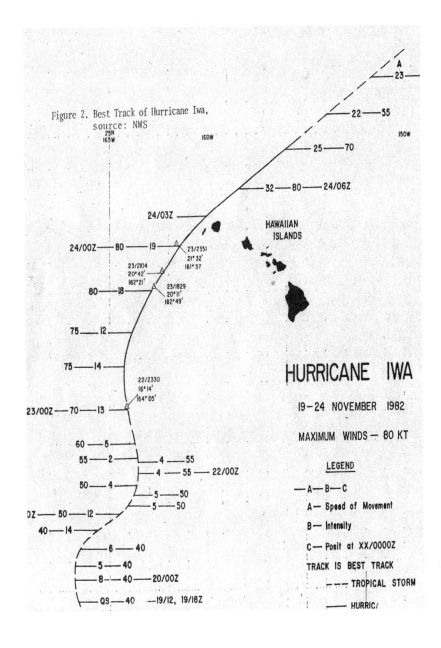

Figure 2. Best Track of Hurricane Iwa,
source: NWS

25N
165W

160W

150W

A
23

22 — 55

25 — 70

32 — 80 — 24/06Z

24/03Z

HAWAIIAN
ISLANDS

24/00Z — 80 — 19

23/2351
21°32'
161°37

23/2104
20°42'
162°21'

23/1829
20°11'
162°49'

80 — 18

75 — 12

75 — 14

22/2330
16°14'
164°05'

23/00Z — 70 — 13

60 — 6

55 — 2

4 — 55

4 — 55 — 22/00Z

50 — 4

5 — 50

5 — 50

0Z — 50 — 12

40 — 14

6 — 40

5 — 40

8 — 40 — 20/00Z

QS — 40 — 19/12, 19/18Z

HURRICANE IWA

19–24 NOVEMBER 1982

MAXIMUM WINDS – 80 KT

LEGEND

— A — B — C

A — Speed of Movement

B — Intensity

C — Posit at XX/0000Z

TRACK IS BEST TRACK

- - - TROPICAL STORM

——— HURRIC/

**Figure 5.1 Best track of Hurricane Iwa. Source: The National
Weather Service**

63

Kauai's children were already in school and their parents were on their way to work. Kauai's mayor, Eduardo Malapit, closed all county offices, allowing everyone to go home except for emergency personnel (Figure 5.1).

On the morning of Tuesday, November 23, 1982, Waimea businessman Mike Faye, manager of Kikiaola Land Company, woke up to a telephone call from his mother-in-law. According to records from the U.S. Army Corps of Engineers, Iwa's storm surge would soon flood the coast from Poipu to Kekaha, with inundated areas extending to 600 feet inland, and Faye's property was not exempt. The flooding he describes was caused by a rise in sea level, resulting from low barometric pressure in the storm's center and by winds directed by the route of the storm's movement .

> "My mother-in-law told us a hurricane was coming. I told her, 'Don't worry. Hurricanes never get us.' When the wind started to increase drastically, I decided I'd better get up and go check on the workmen. Outside, the winds were picking up. The men fueled the chain saws and all our trucks and tractors. We parked the equipment where we thought it would be safe.
>
> "As the winds steadily increased, we all began to realize something bad was going to happen. I sent my wife and baby boy to her parents' house in Kalaheo. She cooked me some chicken and I grabbed all the beer I could find in the refrigerator, still hoping maybe nothing would happen. I had an old Model A Ford pickup parked alongside the big house. I decided to move it to higher ground. If I hadn't, it would have been wiped out.
>
> "When the water started coming up, David Smith, Dickie Vidinha and I jumped into the biggest vehicle we had--a dump truck--and drove through the coconut grove. Coconuts were flying all over the

64

Figure 5.2. A VW floated around the vicinity of the Waimea Plantation Cottages' coconut grove before coming to rest here after the storm surge subsided. *Photo by Mike Faye.

place. We watched the big house garage being torn off by the water and float away, along with all the propane gas cylinders. There were six to eight feet of water inundation on the beachfront and in all the rental cottages. We watched the wind and water move my Hilo sampan car, which was parked in the garage, 200 feet.

"Driving down to another area, we watched a Volkswagen Bug float out of its garage, then the garage fell down and floated away, finally smashing into a clump of trees (Figure 5.2). In our area, the water damage from Iwa was not from crashing waves, but from a wall of water. It gently floated things around, relocating them (Figure 5.3).

"After the eye passed, when the wind changed direction, it caused a flood of water to wash back out to sea. That's when we lost a lot of possessions.

* All photos in Chapter Five are courtesy of Mike Faye unless otherwise specified.

65

Figure 5.3 Iwa wrecked trees, cars and homes. The most extensive damage was caused by the storm surge.

We lost almost all of our wedding gifts which weren't yet unpacked. We lost virtually everything. Our house is three feet off the ground and the water came up four feet. The windows were blown out, even on the mauka side. The day after the storm, while I was inspecting the damage, cows from the dairy farm next door were walking inside the house on two feet of sand."

Kauai's Superintendent of Schools issued a directive on Tuesday, November 23, closing elementary and secondary schools at noon and 12:30 p.m. respectively.

County officials contacted Red Cross personnel and evacuation shelters opened quickly across the island to serve a portion of the 38,856 Kauai residents.

Civil Defense officials sounded sirens at 12:15 p.m. and again at 1 and 2 p.m. At the time of the final soundings, Lihue Airport recorded gusts of 39 mph and coastal flooding

Figure 5.4 Entrance to Waimea Plantation Cottages and dairy before Hurricane Iwa.

Figure 5.5 Same entrance to Waimea Plantation Cottages and dairy after Hurricane Iwa.

had become serious. Roads were impassable by mid-afternoon due to surging waves, downed utility poles and fallen trees.

Police ordered cars off the roads, and KUAI radio station lost power when high winds toppled its tower. Lihue Airport closed at 2:25 p.m., and shuttles took tourists awaiting flights off Kauai to Lihue War Memorial Convention Hall. Tourists at Poipu walked or rode buses to the Koloa shelter (Koloa Elementary School) three-and-a-half miles inland.

Civil Defense officials ordered police officers to seek shelter by 2:30 p.m., as conditions deteriorated quickly. The peak wind speeds hit Lihue between 4 and 8 p.m. and measured 45 knots, gusting to 69 knots (65 mph), as the hurricane's eye passed about 30 miles to the northwest of Kauai. The emergency broadcast station, KIPO, lost its antenna about 5:12 p.m. and resumed broadcasting at 6 p.m., but only with thirty percent of normal broadcasting power.

The worst damage occurred within 130 miles of Iwa's eye (Figures 5.4, 5.5, and 5.6). Roads became impassable as trees, utility poles and wires blocked the major traffic arteries. Kauai's Civil Defense Emergency Operations Center in the basement of the County Building, built in 1913, housed emergency crews, who reported feeling wind-induced tremors in the building and who could hear doors and windows in the upper floors banging relentlessly.

Ocean waves at Poipu, now Kauai's premier resort area, became progressively more threatening over the course of the day. Before dawn, the waves were hitting the sea wall; by mid-morning 12- to 17-foot waves reached homes; at 1 :45 p.m. 24 foot waves assaulted the shore, then, finally at 5 p.m., monstrous 30 foot breakers devastated resort properties and finished destroying what luxurious, beach-front homes remained. Iwa was much stronger before it brushed Kauai, which explains the severe wave damage.

Julie Haviland never expected to encounter a hurricane on the Eden-like Kauai. As a relative newcomer on the

Figure 5.6. Main street in Waimea and former site of "Wrangler's' "Restaurant. (Note small sign in the middle of the rubble).

island, Haviland was inclined to believe the locals when they said that Kauai was essentially immune to hurricanes.

> *"People weren't leery about a hurricane. Everybody went to work and carried on with business as usual. I went to work, knowing there was a possibility of a hurricane, but everyone said, 'The hurricanes get close, but then they turn away from Kauai.' I worked at the YWCA Women's Shelter. Sirens were going off and we needed to get the people at the shelter back to their own homes so they could take care of them. I spent most of the day driving people home. Then I couldn't get home to Poipu. The tree tunnel was blocked with shredded, fallen trees. I spent the night at the shelter with a lot of scared women and children, listening to the radio until it went out. The next morning my boyfriend came to get me in a four-wheel drive. In the daylight, when I saw the island devastated, it hurt. I thought about how the people born and raised on this island must be feeling."*

Offshore and harbor structures designed to withstand high wave forces performed well except for the small boat harbor at Port Allen, where Hurricane Iwa destroyed or sank 44 of 45 civilian boats. Adjacent commercial buildings at the west side port suffered heavy damage or collapsed.

§§§§§

Keith Robinson, who never even heard the hurricane warning, captained the only civilian boat that survived Iwa's wrath.

"I was on my fishing boat, the 'Lehua', a hand-built 31-foot Monterey Motor Sailer. I was vaguely aware there was a tropical storm named Iwa 500 miles to the south, but I had no idea it had suddenly picked up steam and was coming right at us. I'd been on an overnight fishing trip that started around midnight. The moon was setting late and I wanted to do a few hours of akule fishing.

"Iwa came in like a trade wind. I mistook it for one of those localized fall gales that I often fish in. It started at 35 knot winds, waves, and spray. My boat was solid, so I wasn't worried and kept fishing. Along about four or five in the morning, the wind was getting awfully strong... maybe 40-45 knots.

"Just as day was breaking, I hauled in my fishing lines and started for home. That's when I discovered that the boat wasn't making any headway. The stabilizing sail wasn't properly tied and I was terrified the ropes would tear loose. The lee side, which is normally four feet off the water, was already within 18 inches off the water so she was laying way over already. Even under a tiny piece of sail, Port Allen was a long, three-hour haul up the coast.

"Passing Burns Field in 15-20 foot seas, and 50-

60 mph winds, I finally entered the harbor. I was the last boat to enter. The harbor was quiet, only 20-30 mph winds. As I prepared to tie the 'Lehua', I realized the ocean was already developing a lot of power. I decided I'd better get out of the small boat harbor in case it became a death trap. I maneuvered the boat out into the open part of the small boat harbor and kept sailing around. It was a very, very unpleasant experience. At 1 :30 p.m., I had to shift from the Nawiliwili side of the pier, because the wind was so strong I couldn't control the boat anymore. With the surf chaotic and waves 10 to 20 feet high, I had no choice but to go around in circles. A Navy target boat had broken loose and I kept trying to avoid hitting it. By now, there was a huge slick of debris from smashed boats. The debris entered the engine intake and was plugging up my raw water filter. I was trapped right up against the shoreline in all those breakers. At about 4 p.m. in the afternoon, after sailing all day, I noticed that the wind had changed direction. To me, that was the first sign that I might live. I'd hoped to run the boat ashore if things got real bad so I could walk away. But, it seemed doubtful anyone could survive waves like that (Figure 5.7).

"Watching the small boat harbor go was like watching a Hollywood disaster movie. Boats piling on top of each other, on top of the wharf. . . boats, buildings and roofs flying away. Huge waves breaking under the wharf thrust compressed air in huge spouts and spray. It was quite a show. Turning away to check the engine temperature, I noticed that it was very hot. I knew in about three minutes the engine could catch on fire and the engine oil might vaporize and explode. My only choice was to point the boat right at the main freighter dock, the only thing left in the harbor, and try to make it. At pre-

Figure 5.7 Keith Robinson stands aboard the *Lehua*, the fishing boat he made himself and used for commercial fishing purposes. The *Lehua* was the only civilian boat at Port Allen Harbor during Iwa that was not destroyed. (Photo by author).

cisely that moment, the rudder jammed. I had no steering. Luckily, Lehua's bow was pointed in the right direction and she just nosed up against the dock.

"My brother, Bruce, and some of the Niihau men had been taking shelter on the dock for hours, which was very generous of them. Glass skylights were blowing off a 30-foot roof above the main wharf. These huge pieces of glass would hit the concrete, fly up 6 to 7 feet, and blow away in 100 mph wind. I n 110 mph gusts, they ran out just as the boat was nosing up against the pier and secured the boat. When they finished tying the ropes, they walked off and left me. I yelled at them to come back. But, *they couldn't hear me. I knew the battle to save the boat was just beginning. Luckily there was a half moon so there was some light coming through the clouds. Around 7 p.m., I could see that the bow line was nearly chafed through. I had another line but there was no one on the dock to throw it to. The only thing to do was to wait until one of the 10- to 15 -foot waves lifted the boat level with the dock and jump--with a load of rope in my hands in 100 mph wind. If I miscalculated my jump, I'd fall into the space between the boat and dock and be squashed. I didn't jump far enough. Now I was swimming in the water in my sea boots and full regalia with rope all over my face. The boat was being flung against the dock every few seconds. When I could reach the chafed rope, I made a wild lunge for it. The boat snapped away and the rope tightened like a bowstring. After two more attempts, I was catapulted onto the dock. When I tied the rope and turned to jump back on the boat, I was so exhausted, I tripped over my own feet. Again, falling head first into the water, I climbed out like a drowned rat. The next morning dawned bright and clear. Finally, I looked about. There was nothing left of the small boat harbor but a little bit of rubble sticking out of the ocean. Everything had been destroyed. My boat was the only boat afloat."*

Kauai fire fighters were finally able to begin search and rescue operations as winds subsided, and while Robinson slept in exhausted bouts during the night, looters helped themselves to fishing reels and electronic equipment from the wrecked boats. Looting also became a problem in the affluent Poipu area. As darkness enveloped the island, reports of looting reached officials. At 8:40 p.m., Governor George Ariyoshi called out the National Guard, and soldiers began patrolling the streets by 9:30 p.m.

By 11 p.m., Tuesday, November 23, Iwa departed, and National Weather Service officials canceled the hurricane warning and watch.

Remarkably, no deaths occurred on Kauai from Hurricane Iwa. Human injuries consisted of cuts from flying glass, and one man suffered a broken leg when he fell from his roof during the storm.

The worst damages on Kauai were due to Iwa's raging wind and hammering surf. Blocked roadways, power outages, sporadic telephone service, and a noticeable lack of radio broadcasts paralyzed Kauai. Downed communication systems, such as microwave antenna towers and commercial radio antennas, limited the operation of telephones and radio station transmissions. About forty percent of the island's phones were dead, and even Kauai's Civil Defense Agency lost its National Warning System and teletype links due to the power failure, but regained communication by switching to emergency generators.

Gas station pumps were inoperable because of the lack of electricity. In the few stores that opened for business in the wake of Iwa, residents scrambled to buy camping gear, kerosene and roofing supplies.

In the days following the hurricane, Governor Ariyoshi and the State Civil Defense Director executed a statewide disaster declaration based on reports supplied by FEMA survey teams. By Thanksgiving Day, November 26, the Small Business Administration, the Red Cross, the Army Corps of Engineers, and other federal agencies arrived on Kauai. Their assessments were reported to President Ronald Reagan, who, on November 27, declared Hawaii a disaster area. A week later, on December 2, disaster application centers opened at Koloa, Lihue and Kilauea.

While Iwa caused irreparable property damage, it also uncovered a glimpse of Kauai's ancient history. Along the Princeville shoreline, a stretch of beach below Pali Ke Kua washed away, uncovering previously undiscovered petroglyphs carved on a large slab of sandstone. The arti-

Figure 5. 8 Once the rains and storm surge receded, a variety of household items ended up caught in trees and bushes.

fact was documented by the Bishop Museum when it first appeared in 1983, but has since been reclaimed by the shifting sands.

Iwa's damage to Kauai

Sixty percent of Kauai's hotel units were damaged or destroyed. The most heavily damaged areas were Poipu and Princeville, where beachfront hotel rooms crumbled like castles made of sand. Many Poipu Beach resorts, the centurions of Kauai's booming economy, suffered severe damage from flooding and wave action. The Sheraton Kauai sustained the greatest loss. Waves ripped through oceanfront units in one wing of the hotel, leaving only a foundation slab, and another wing teetered precariously on the eroded beach. Waves inundated Poipu's roads and parking areas, submerging approximately forty cars at the Waiohai Resort. Searching for higher ground, hotel maintenance workers pushed the floating cars around the parking lot.

The first floor of the Waiohai remained under water for several days. Wave, sand and boulder damage destroyed all the landscaping and ocean-side rooms on the ground level. Eight feet of water, two-and-a-half feet of sand and numerous one-ton boulders filled the basement, which housed the laundry, kitchen and electrical center.

Storm surge and waves severely eroded the reinforced concrete Kuhio Shores condominiums and gutted the first floor. In Poipu, million-dollar beachfront homes were torn from their foundations and washed inland, leaving only concrete slabs. The Beach House Restaurant, popular with locals and visitors alike, splintered and succumbed to a watery grave. Along the south shore, Iwa's debris line extended up to 300 yards inland.

At Princeville, 127 out of 180 new condominiums and town houses were damaged, and Hanalei Bay Villas suffered extensive damage. In Hanalei, Ching Young Store and the Hanalei Colony Resort also suffered damage.

On Kauai's west side, beach houses in Kekaha also sustained heavy damage from the storm surge. As in the two previous hurricanes, the storm surge undermined significant portions of Kekaha's coastal Highway 50, carrying away chunks of pavement and blocking the main route to and from the Pacific Missile Range Facility in Mana. Poipu Road, Hoone Road, Puolo Road, and Lawai Road on the south siide also sustained major damage.

Hurricane shelters did not fare well, either. In Lihue, at the War Memorial Convention Center, wind shattered the large glass doors in the lobby.

At Kapaa High School, four classroom buildings lost portions of their roofs, and in the crowded cafeteria, the glass windows blew in. The Bali Hai Restaurant of the Hanalei Bay Resort, also used as a shelter, sustained roof damage and the sliding glass doors exploded. Luckily, the only injuries were cuts.

All of Kauai's 14 schools were damaged, six of which

sustained more than $200,000 worth of damage. Kauai High School and Kauai Community College suffered the greatest losses. The recently constructed, county-owned Vidinha and Hanapepe Stadium complexes, the Wailua Golf Course, Salt Pond and Poipu beach parks suffered extensive damages.

The Lihue Airport sustained damage, and the state-owned Nawiliwili Harbor's commercial piers--the hub of Kauai's import and export business--were severely damaged. Kikiaola Harbor was destroyed, along with Port Allen Harbor, which suffered the greatest loss.

Kauai's lifelines, including power, water and communications, were badly damaged. Of Kauai Electric's 600 miles of transmission and distribution lines, consisting of mostly overhead lines supported by wooden poles, 200 miles fell because of the high velocity winds.

With electrical power disrupted, water couldn't be pumped from several reservoirs to the Wailua, Kapaa and Hanalei communities. The armed forces and other government agencies shipped generators from Oahu to Kauai to restore some of the pumps, while other residents received fresh water from tanker trucks stationed at neighborhood centers.

The Navy and utility crews from other islands assisted Kauai Electric Company and Hawaiian Telephone in repairing power and telephone lines so that regular services could resume. By Christmas, power was restored to nearly all areas of Kauai except Kokee. Kauai Electric Company's physical damage topped $3.5 million and officials estimated $3 million in lost revenues.

FEMA reported in 1982 that a total of 1,944 homes on Kauai were damaged and of that figure, 339 homes were completely destroyed. The worst residential damages occurred in Poipu, Lihue, Wailua Homesteads, Kalaheo, Kekaha, and Princeville. Final estimates placed Iwa's statewide damages at $234 million, one third of which occurred on Kauai. Utilities suffered millions of dollars in damages.

Nearly half of the land used for growing sugar and other crops suffered catastrophic damage. Vegetable, fruit and poultry farmers also sustained heavy losses. Upland forests suffered extensive loss of trees and vegetation, and this habitat destruction affected native birds and insects.

Iwa's Damage on Oahu

On Oahu, strong, damaging winds arrived approximately 30 to 60 minutes later than on Kauai, which allowed more time for people in danger zones to evacuate and for emergency personnel to prepare. The direct effects of Iwa on Oahu were confined to roughly twenty percent of the population, particularly those living near the west, east and south coast and in the Wahiawa-Schofield Barracks region. Iwa pounded the Waianae Coast with savage surf, then its winds accelerated over the Koolau and Waianae mountain ranges, causing some damage to the windward side of Oahu. One thousand people living in low-lying areas had to evacuate their homes, and sporadic power outages plagued Oahu for several days.

Aboard the U.S. Navy ship, the Goldsborough, a sailor vanished overboard when a 30-foot wave slammed into the ship's deck during the hurricane's rampage. The unfortunate seaman, Jose Cantu suffered a broken neck, and five other crewmen were injured. The six crewmen had been on anchor detail near the front of the ship when the wave struck.

At the Honolulu International Airport, strong winds rolled an old DC-3 across the airfield. A massive plate glass window shattered inward on passengers who were waiting to board flights. Although sprayed with broken glass, these lucky travelers received no major injuries. When the power at the airport failed, emergency standby power was sufficient only for aircraft control and safety operations.

The National Weather Service and the Central Pacific Hurricane Center housed in the main terminal of Honolulu International Airport also lost power at the height of the storm. For a short time, satellite coverage of Hurricane Iwa was lost.

Military bases were not exempt from Iwa's ravages. Schofield Barracks suffered $30 million in damages, as did a housing area at Fort Kamehameha, next to Hickam Air Force Base. In Waikiki, Fort DeRussy was inundated by high surf.

At Aloha Towers, condominium tenants were evacuated because building designers had not planned for the possibility of a direct-hit hurricane and some feared that the building would collapse in the high winds. Of all Oahu's homes, 126 were destroyed and 437 were severely damaged. Heavy crop damage was reported on Oahu's western shore.

While Kauai should have been more prepared than Oahu, with two hurricanes' worth of experience under her belt, the rapidly developing Garden Island was not. Along with the boom in development came contractors and builders who hadn't considered hurricane-force fortification for their structures. And, of the many local residents who had to rebuild their homes and businesses after Nina and Dot, most did so economically--but not necessarily safely--with the help of friends and family.

Oahu residents and officials, on the other hand, should have learned from Kauai's experiences and should have been better prepared. In its 1983 report on Hurricane Iwa, the Committee on Natural Disasters claimed, "Iwa may be the largest economic disaster to be suffered by the state in this century."

The Lessons of Iwa

The public's most often expressed complaint about Hurricane Iwa was that warnings were insufficient. Residents cited a discrepancy between the hurricane warnings issued by various agencies and their own perceived or experienced threat. Residents also claimed that the warnings issued by the National Weather Service did not coincide with the warnings issued by Kauai or Oahu's Civil Defense officials. A forecast error was blamed for the time lapse between the initial detection of Iwa and the warning of threatened populations, according to the 1983 Committee on Natural Disas-

Figure 5. 9 Some coconut palms were able to weather the storm. But telephone and electrical lines did not fare so well.

ters report.

On Oahu, the National Weather Service issued a hurricane watch rather than a warning because some parts of the island wouldn't be affected. The warning sirens couldn't be activated independently only for exposed areas, so the National Weather Service chose to rely on the police and Civil Defense officials to warn residents.

At the Honolulu City Council's single public hearing to review Hurricane Iwa, Waianae residents alleged that Civil Defense officials issued warnings too late because they were understaffed and complained about the lack of safe evacuation routes that should have been established. Evacuation plans for Oahu's many tourists were also lacking.

On Kauai, although the hurricane watch was issued on Monday night, most residents were asleep. The following morning's hurricane warning upgrade preceded the hurricane by only a few hours and gave residents very little time to prepare. Schoolchildren were endangered because they were released from school between noon and 12:30 p.m. and reached home later still.

On Kauai, approximately 15,000 people were accommodated in public shelters, including unexpectedly large numbers of visitors. Some of the shelters were not safe and lacked bedding and food. None of Kauai's public shelters offered definitive protection against hurricane-force winds. The result was extensive roof damage at the Kilauea Neighborhood Center, Kapaa and Waimea High Schools, and at the Lihue War Memorial Convention Center, where plate glass doors blew in.

The statewide Emergency Broadcast System received its first real test during Hurricane Iwa. A large flaw emerged quickly. The system depended on electrical power and a functional telephone system to operate at peak efficiency. When these became inoperable due to the storm, back-up equipment and generators were difficult to obtain. At one point during the storm, all radio and television stations lost power on Oahu, with the exception of a religious station, KAIM. Civil Defense officials interrupted a sermon to broadcast hurricane warning bulletins. Loss of Oahu radio stations impaired public safety efforts on both Kauai and Oahu, because Kauai's radio stations were out and residents sought information from Oahu stations. Battery-powered radios on Oahu could only pick up commercial radio stations on Maui. Listeners reported that Maui radio stations were oblivious to what was happening on Kauai and Oahu, and they offered no guidance or instruction to Kauai or Oahu hurricane victims who had no other means of receiving information. Confusion prevailed about road conditions, utilities and the status of schools.

Kauai's business owners loved the tourists, but once the tourists were on Kauai , very little had been done in making provisions for them in the event of a natural disaster. The need for adequate shelters to house the visitor plant and the provisions for mass feeding were inadequate. Other problems included the lack of temporary housing, public reticence in receiving federal aid and the complex procedures necessary for determining wind versus water damage for insurance reimbursements. Finally, many residents cited that mainland disaster workers displayed little sensitivity to the local residents' cultural practices.

After Iwa struck Kauai, it was obvious that serious social and economic impacts could occur, particularly along shoreline development areas. The island's 5,207 hotel units were all in coastal areas. Most of the damage occurred to shorefront resorts on Kauai's south coast and homes along the coastal fringe. Although sustained winds, except for gusts, remained below hurricane force of 74 mph, substandard construction, poor design and inadequate building codes offered a plausible explanation for the extensive damage wrought by Iwa.

Additionally, the narrow ribbon of highway connecting Kauai's communities was easily disrupted. Before Hurricane Iwa, Kauai officials had no post-disaster redevelopment plan. Public officials and private businesses and residential owners sought rapid reconstruction with existing codes and regulations, as they were the only guidelines. Kauai's residents needed roofs in a hurry and businesses needed to get back to normal operations as quickly as possible.

After witnessing the three tempests that shook Kauai and nicked Oahu, scientists and government officials finally recognized how dangerous hurricanes could be. In a 1993 report by Professor Thomas Schoeder, Iwa's damages greatly outweighed those of Dot, 23 years earlier.

"Primary losses were no longer suffered by agriculture but by the tourism industry which had developed since statehood, and by the substantially larger 1982 population. Surge and overwash on the south shore of Kauai exceeded the 100-year inundation levels developed for tsunamis."

In a 1983 Hurricane Iwa report, the Committee on Natural Disasters concluded that the entire state could be vulnerable to hurricanes and that rescue operations could be thwarted because of the Hawaiian Islands' isolation. The report's author concluded that, "Iwa was not even a strong hurricane, hence the extent of the damage caused becomes all the more disconcerting."

Although the Committee was unsettled, little was done to rectify the situation. According to a 1993 report prepared by Arthur Chiu, et al., comparisons of damages that occurred during each hurricane were analyzed. This report concluded that recommendations by the 1982 mitigation committee were largely ignored.

Following the clean up in the aftermath of a natural disaster, which to that date had been the worst in the state's history, Kauai was again set to experience the growing pains and the concurrent prosperity of rapid development.

Politician Tony Kunimura, who had defeated minimal-development advocate JoAnn Yukimura in the 1982 mayor's race, was ushered into office on Hurricane Iwa's tailwinds. Iwa created a short-term economic disaster across the island which led to heightened support of development. Eager to promote the economic and emotional stability of Kauai's people, Kunimura ingeniously let Iwa pave the way for even more development.

By the mid-1980s, Mayor Kunimura initiated two innovative techniques for luring tourists back to Kauai in the aftermath of Iwa -- the 'Kauai Loves You' advertising campaign, and the Visitor's Ambassador program. These endeavors brought more than a lion's share of visitors streaming back to the Garden Island in the mid-1980s, and Kauai soon witnessed the highest visitor counts in its history.

Tourism boomed as a result of an affluent world economy and, during Kunimura's tenure, Kauai County, for the first time in its history, appropriated funds for tourist promotion. Former Kauai County Councilman Jimmy Tehada explained.

"When I came on board in December 1986, we were pulling out of a recession. The economy was improving, the Hyatt was being built, and the Westin was coming on board. We still didn't have that much

much money in the budget until we got the state to give us the tourist accommodation tax."

As Kauai's mayor from 1982 until 1988, Kunimura took the reins of a rapidly developing island with an economy that glittered like gold. Realizing that Kauai had limited 59 opportunities for economic growth, he focused on tourism to bolster the economy. While the Hawaii Visitors Bureau was tapping the European market, Kunimura--who was fluent in the Japanese language--pursued the Japanese market and enticed Japanese visitors to increase the duration of their stay on Kauai from a single day to extended overnighters.

Kunimura was reelected as Kauai's mayor again in 1984 and 1986. During this period, Kauai experienced the highest rate and level of economic and population growth in the island's history. Million-dollar projects, including Kukui Grove Shopping Center, the Kauai Hilton (Nukolii development) and the Westin at Kalapaki, were operational and providing more jobs than could be filled by local residents.

Although damaged during Iwa's rampage, hotels had been repaired and thrived as tourists streamed onto the island. Properties including the Hanalei Colony Resort, the Hanalei Bay Resort, the Waiohai, and the Sheraton Kauai hosted record numbers of visitors.

Kauai's resident population during the development heyday of the late 1980s continued to increase at twice the rate of the rest of the state. Although Kauai was the smallest of the four counties in the state, its growth rate had been the second fastest in the state over the decade, second only to Maui, and twice as fast as the state average.

With a boom in population to service the growing economy, residential projects struggled to keep pace. Kunimura's rigorous economic expansion program resulted in a serious lack of affordable housing and accompanying infrastructure for those who came to Kauai to live and work.

To meet these demands, the second phase of the Princeville expansion commenced and major subdivision developments by A&B and Amfac were built. Dennis Oliver, who was active in Kauai's Democratic party, explained the situation:

"Though we were expanding, the county had to provide more police and fire services, the roadways were clogged and housing rental rates were going up. The quality of life was being threatened because the infrastructure didn't come close to meeting the needs of the growing island."

Dissatisfied with the rampant growth and the lack of infrastructure to support it, Kauai's residents were ready for a change in leadership. In 1988, Kauai residents chose an avenue of "slow growth" and a mayor who promised just that. In this peculiar twist of fate, JoAnn Yukimura, who had long opposed the very development that Kunimura endorsed, finally won the mayoral race with the highest number of votes for one candidate ever recorded in a Kauai election.

Yukimura was determined to address the lightning rod issues that accompanied the rapid development of the Kunimura administration. She did so by making plans to build the Poipu bypass road, acquire the Lihue Shopping Center for Kauai's civic center, install a sewage system for rapidly-growing Kapaa, and get affordable housing projects on line.

Although the memory of Hurricane Iwa had nearly faded from the island's collective consciousness by the end of the decade, development-wary Kauai residents ushered in the '90s economically optimistic and ready to relax on the '80s remaining wave of prosperity. Residents and visitors to the Garden Island were unaware that the stage was being set again for island-wide devastation, only this time the bowling ball would be a great deal larger, and there would be far more pins in its path.

§§§§§

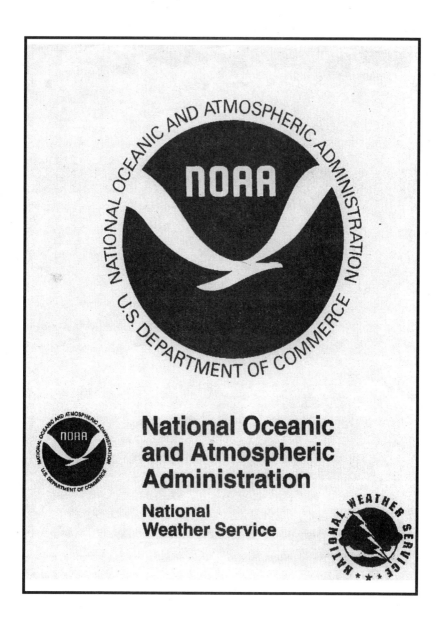

National Oceanic and Atmospheric Administration

National
Weather Service

Chapter Six

Defending Against the Winds

The destruction wrought by Hurricane Iwa was impressive, yet the storm's death toll remained minimal. Three factors contributed to the low mortality rate. Weather forecasting was becoming more accurate, the public warning systems were improving, and plans for sheltering and providing mass care began to be addressed. Military intervention in the immediate post-disaster period also became an option.

Since the beginning of time, man has been affected by severe changes in his environment. To the ancient hunter-gathers, crop-growers and farmers over the millennia, extreme weather conditions have heralded death and destruction as well as life and renewal. Just as man evolved in surroundings fraught with dangers from the natural environment, he developed ways to help him prepare for, and anticipate inclement conditions. Over the years, many people contributed to advents in technology, so that more lives could be saved and damages minimized through the advanced techniques of weather warning systems.

Early Meteorologists

Fascinated by weather patterns and climate, some influential early Americans made the first contributions to modern-day weather forecasting. These men included George Washington, Ben Franklin, and Thomas Jefferson. Washington and Jefferson both contributed to meteorological science by recording detailed weather observations from their homes in Virginia, a state regularly visited by passing tropical storms.

Benjamin Franklin's interest in meteorology and ocean

ography led him to his famous investigation of atmospheric electricity using a kite. Franklin also conducted extensive studies of the north Atlantic Ocean's Gulf Stream current.

Present-day Weather Service storm warnings are based on standard knowledge about storms and their motions that came from the research of early pioneers in the field of meteorology. William Redfield, a marine engineer from Connecticut, first discovered the counterclockwise circulation within storms after studying the orientation of fallen trees on Long Island after an 1821 hurricane. He postulated that centrifugal force was important in keeping the motion circular and counterclockwise around a low-pressure center. Other early American scientists, among them Elias Loomis, pioneered studies of individual storms and produced primitive weather maps.

It was not until the 19th century, however, that weather observations were systematically recorded to help scientists understand recurring weather patterns. While European scientists contributed to pioneering work in meteorology, Americans were leaders in the 19th century's understanding of weather forecasting and storm knowledge. With its extremes in weather, from tornadoes to hurricanes to blizzards, North America's climate stimulated meteorological interest and the quest for more information.

An unlikely group established one of the first weather observation programs in North America in 1820. Army Medical Corps doctors, who possessed accurate thermometers and who were experienced in keeping comprehensive records, took weather observations at military forts across the continent. Their records proved of great value to the Quartermaster Corps for planning missions and supplying the troops.

In the 1830s, James Espy of Philadelphia's Franklin Institute initiated an extensive volunteer weather observation program, which developed into the Smithsonian Institution's observer network in the 1840s. About the same time, the Naval Observatory initiated an observer network in coastal areas.

Its director, Matthew Maury, supervised the collection of shipboard weather observations from all over the world. Entries in ship's logbooks were gleaned for weather data, and crew members were encouraged to make observations on standardized forms. Maury exchanged this data with other maritime nations and compiled extensive climatological summaries and charts of winds, weather and ocean storms.

In the Crimean War of 1853, both English and French fleets sank in the Black Sea during a terrible storm that was traced back to the Mediterranean Sea a day or two earlier. Because the loss of life was so great, the public demanded to know why there was no warning. In response to this public outcry, both countries began to develop their own weather services.

The History of the National Weather Service

In the United States, heavy losses to shipping on the Great Lakes instigated another weather service operation. Increase Lapham, a member of the Signal Corps in Wisconsin, secured support from the National Board of Trade and the U.S. Congress for a federal weather service to help predict storms on the Great Lakes and along America's coasts. Lapham sent his first forecast from Chicago on November 1, 1870, and the National Weather Service was born.

The organized compilation of important weather data led to the establishment of an agency that would eventually become one of the foremost authorities on weather interpretation and prediction in the world. From humble beginnings, the National Weather Service grew into a vital public service agency. Its mission--to forecast the weather and alert both civilians and the military to weather that could threaten or destroy lives and property--has been the agency's driving force since its inception.

The "new" National Weather Service of 1870 was a branch of the Army's Signal Service, which also operated telegraph lines. Following the development of the telegraph and radio, it was possible to quickly collect data, construct weather charts and provide prompt reports, even from ships out at sea. Based on these charts, warnings about approaching storms could be issued.

The Weather Bureau became a civilian agency in 1890 under the auspices of the Department of Agriculture, mainly because of dissatisfaction with weather forecasting under the military. The hurricane of 1875 that destroyed Indianola, Texas, without much warning was a predisposing factor.

It was not until the Spanish-American War of 1898 that an effort was made to establish a comprehensive hurricane warning service. President William McKinley stated that he was more afraid of a hurricane than he was of the Spanish Navy. He extended the warning service to include warnings for shipping interests as well as the military. Before that, hurricane warnings were only issued for the United States coastal areas. Hurricane warning stations were established throughout the West Indies. A forecast center was established in Kingston, Jamaica, and later moved to Havana, Cuba, in 1899. Soon after, the warning service was extended to Mexico and Central America.

The infamous Galveston hurricane of 1900 -- called the greatest natural disaster in America's history -- killed 6,000 people. Because there was no formal hurricane warning system in place at the time, this calamity prompted the transfer of the warning service to Washington, DC, where it remained until 1935.

During the 1920s, poorly reported hurricanes ravaged the U.S. In 1926, a strong hurricane devastated Miami and Ft. Lauderdale, as well as most of southeastern Florida, and caused more than 200 deaths. Warnings for that storm were issued at night when most residents were asleep and unaware of the danger. In 1928, a very severe hurricane hit south Florida and killed an estimated 1,800 people who drowned when Lake Okeechobee overflowed. The year 1933 heralded a record of 21 tropical storms. Because of inadequate forecasting and insufficient public notification, that year, nine hurricanes and two tropical storms decimated the

East Coast. Then, in 1934, the D.C. Weather Service flubbed a forecast and warning for an approaching hurricane in the very shell-shocked Galveston area.

Those incidents led Congress and the President to revamp and decentralize the hurricane warning service. Improvements included 24-hour operations with teletypewriter hook-ups along the Gulf and Atlantic coasts; weather observations at 6-hour intervals; hurricane advisories at least four times a day; and a more adequate upper-air observation network. New hurricane forecast centers were established at Jacksonville, Florida; New Orleans, Louisiana; San Juan, Puerto Rico; and Boston, Massachusetts. In the same year, 1940, along with the advent of civil aviation, the National Weather Service was transferred from the Department of Agriculture to the Department of Commerce.

More improvements were forthcoming. In 1943, the primary hurricane forecast office at Jacksonville moved to Miami, where the Weather Bureau established a joint hurricane warning service with the Army Air Corps and the Navy.

World War II technology contributed significantly to the understanding of weather changes and the variation in wind circulation patterns at high altitudes versus those near the earth's surface. Although information of this sort was classified, leaps and bounds were made in analyzing atmospheric data from aircraft, isolated balloon sensors, mountaintop observations, "radiosones" (specialized balloon-borne weather instruments), and the use of electronic digital computers. Scientists soon discovered the existence of jet streams.

Aircraft reconnaissance also came into play. In 1943, Col. Joseph Duckworth made the first intentional flight into the eye of a hurricane. The following year, the military set a precedent with regular aircraft reconnaissance, providing hurricane forecasters with the location and intensity of population-threatening storms.

Radar used in air defense was often disrupted by reflections from rain clouds. However, this nuisance was turned into an advantage--the creation of weather radar, an important tool for detecting rain-producing clouds and hurricanes.

While Hawaii was still a U.S. Territory and experiencing its own bout of hurricanes, a number of hurricanes struck the East Coast in the 1950s, causing much damage and flooding. Congress responded with increased appropriations to strengthen the warning service and intensify research into hurricanes. The Weather Bureau organized the National Hurricane Research Project under the direction of Dr. Robert H. Simpson. The Air Force and the Navy provided the first aircraft to be used by the project to investigate the structure, characteristics and movement of tropical storms. In 1955, the Miami office was officially designated as the National Hurricane Center and the "satellite era" officially commenced with the launch of the Russian Sputnik, and the American Explorer satellites in the late 1950s.

In 1960, radar capable of "seeing" out to a distance of 200 to 250 miles from their coastal sites were established at strategic locations. The most critical technological development in the history of weather forecasting and hurricane prediction was the launch of the TIROS I (discussed in Chapter Four). With TIROS I in orbit, hurricane forecasters were given the ability to detect storms before they hit land. TIROS I also provided advanced information about the atmosphere's global circulation and the life cycles of hurricanes.

How the Warning System Works

Gone are the days when an embryonic hurricane anywhere in the Pacific (or elsewhere) can escape detection. Earth-orbiting satellites operated by the National Oceanic and Atmospheric Administration (NOAA) keep the earth's atmosphere under constant surveillance. Well before a storm has evolved, scientists at NOAA's National Hurricane Center Office in Honolulu have begun to track the disturbance via the relatively new Geostationary Operational Environmental Satellite (GOES) West.

Meteorologists utilize satellite data coming in from polar-orbiting and geostationary spacecraft as well as reports from ships and planes. Some features that indicate the potential development of a hurricane include cumulus clouds covered by the cirrostratus deck of a highly organized convective system, showers that become steady rains, dropping atmospheric pressure, or intensification of the tradewinds.

If these features develop into a tropical storm, the system gets a name. Naming a storm brings a much more elaborate warning system into play. Meteorologists and public officials cautiously initiate long-distance communication lines and hurricane readiness plans.

As a Pacific hurricane drifts closer to the islands, it comes under surveillance by the National Weather Service's Honolulu Forecast Office's land-based Doppler radar. Each of the four land-based Doppler radar sites in the Hawaiian Islands can detect weather disturbances, precise position, measurements of wind speeds, and rainfall within a radius of 125 miles from the radar site. There are two sites on the Big Island, one on Molokai, and Kauai's site is located in the McBryde coffee fields near Port Allen, Kauai.

Through the hurricane's life-span, advisories from the National Hurricane Center give the storm's position and what the forecasters expect the storm to do. As the hurricane drifts to within a day or two of its predicted landfall, these advisories begin to carry watch and warning messages, telling people when and where the hurricane is expected to strike and what its effects are likely to be. Not until the hurricane has lost speed and intensity, dumped its great cargo of moisture and turned into more benevolent types of weather does the hurricane emergency end.

The hurricane warning system that monitors the Hawaiian Islands is a good one. Considering the low death tolls in both Iwa and Iniki, the system gives adequate advance warning. Hurricane tracking and warning apparatus has greatly improved over the years and will continue to do so. Still, any significant improvements must come from quantum leaps in scientific understanding. The forecasters also know that science will never provide a full solution to the problems of hurricane safety. Rapid development on all of the Hawaiian Islands jeopardizes many people who have sparse experience of hurricanes, whether they're new residents of the state, residents of islands without a history of hurricanes or visitors to the islands. For vulnerable populations, hurricane awareness and preparedness, along with education, will be the key means of saving lives and mitigating property damage.

Luckily, throughout the 1960s and 1970s, National Weather Service officials, including Dr. Robert Simpson and Dr. Neil Frank, placed a renewed emphasis on research and development activities through satellite applications and the development of statistical and dynamic models as forecast aids. They also stressed the need for hurricane preparedness.

James Weyman, the Director of the National Hurricane Center in Honolulu, officiates at a time in history when the National Weather Service's modernization program will lead to more effective warning and forecasting of hurricanes.

Aircraft Reconnaissance

Aerial weather reconnaissance is vitally important to the forecasters of the National Hurricane Center. Reconnaissance aircraft penetrate to the core of the storm and provide detailed measurements of its wind field as well as accurate location of its center information that is usually not available from any other source. This information helps the meteorologist determine what is going on inside a storm as it actually happens. Aircraft data, coupled with data from satellites, buoys, and land and ship reports, makes up an important part of the information available to the hurricane specialists for their forecast of speed, intensity, and direction of movement of the storm.

The National Hurricane Center is supported by specially modified aircraft of the U.S. Air Force Reserve (USAFR) and the National Oceanic and Atmospheric Administration's (NOAA) Aircraft Operations Center (AOC). The USAFR crews are known as the "Storm Trackers" and are part of the

815th Tactical Airlift Squadron which is based at Keesler Air Force Base near Biloxi, Mississippi. They fly the Lockheed WC-1 30 Hercules, a four- engine turboprop aircraft which carries a crew of six people and can stay aloft for up to 14 hours. Additional crews fly the Lockheed WP-3D Orions, another four-engine turboprop that carries a crew consisting of from seven to seventeen persons and can stay aloft for up to 12 hours. These aircraft and crews are based at Miami International Airport. Both units can be deployed as needed in the Atlantic, Caribbean, Gulf of Mexico, and the central Pacific Ocean.

Meteorological information obtained from aerial reconnaissance includes wind speeds, pressure, temperature, dew point temperature, and location of the storm center. A parachute-borne weather sensor dropped from the plane measures the storm characteristics below the aircraft. Data from the storm environment is available as often as once every minute. This information provides a detailed look at the structure of the storm and a clear indication of its intensity.

Flying into a hurricane is a inimitable experience. Weather crew members who have flown combat missions say that their feelings before both missions were similar. There is a blend of excitement and apprehension. Adding to the tension is the knowledge that no two hurricanes are alike. Some are gentle, while others are maniacal. Preparations for flying into a hurricane must be thorough.

All crew members are highly trained specialists. Loose objects are tied down or stowed away, and crew members wear seat belts and safety harnesses. Once the aircraft's radar picks up the storm, the crew determines the easiest way to get inside. In a well-developed storm, this can be a difficult challenge.

Winds at flight level often exceed 100 miles an hour, and the wall cloud surrounding the center (eye) can be several miles thick. Rain often comes in torrents, and updrafts and downdrafts are usually strong and frequent. Inside the eye, however, the conditions are much different; many times the ocean is visible and there are blue skies and sunshine above. The flight level winds are nearly calm. Often the wall cloud presents a stadium effect.

Both the WC-130 Hercules and the WP-3 Orion operate most efficiently at altitudes of 24,000 to 30,000 feet. Since most storms occur some distance from the aircraft's home station, the crew usually flies to the storm as high as they can because this helps to conserve fuel. About 200 miles from the storm, the aircraft descends to its storm operating level.

If the storm is in its infancy, such as a depression or tropical storm with winds less than 50 mph, then the crew operates as close to the surface of the sea as can be done safely--usually about 1,500 feet. If the storm is more fully developed, either a hurricane or a strong tropical storm, then the aircraft flies its pattern, including penetrations to the center, at 10,000 feet altitude.

A typical mission will last from 10 to 12 hours, during which time the crew will penetrate to the center of the storm anywhere from 3 to 6 times. When its mission is completed, the aircraft will climb back to altitude for the trip home.

§§§§§

Chapter Seven

A Sharp and Piercing Wind

In less than a decade after the 1982 Hurricane Iwa, Kauai islanders would find themselves calling on private, public and military factions to provide relief from hurricane winds once again.

While a number of significant weather systems headed toward Kauai but did not make landfall, Kauai's economy also barreled ahead, again without much thought about the consequences of increased development and the impact that hurricanes might have on the increasing infra- structure.

In 1983, tropical storms Gil and Narda approached and skirted the islands without any damage or catastrophe. Gil passed within 10 miles of Kauai's north shore at noon on August 3, 1983, with localized heavy rains and high surf that pounded the northeast shores of Kauai and Oahu.

Hurricane Raymond barreled toward the Big Island on October 14, 1983. Bigger and stronger than Hurricane Iwa, the storm posed a real threat to the Hawaiian Islands when it approached dangerously close--only several hundred miles east of the Big Island.

Civil Defense chief Sonny Gerardo urged Kauai resi- dents to begin preparing for the storm. However, Raymond changed course and spared the islands. Gerardo said that Raymond was so large that if the eye were centered over Maui, all the Hawaiian Islands would be covered by the storm.

October of 1985 saw a serious threat to Kauai once again. Hurricane Nele mimicked the tracks of Nina and Iwa and brought high surf to the Poipu coastline.

Estelle in July 1986 caused very damaging high surf and heavy rains on the Big Island, while the south shores of

Maui suffered road damage.

Oahu and Kauai again saw a serious threat posed by Hurricane Uleki in September 1988. On approaching the state, Uleki stalled southwest of the islands and brought only heavy rains and high surf to the Big Island. Luckily, when it commenced moving again, Uleki moved westward, away from the islands.

Fefa gained hurricane status well east of the Hawaiian Islands, but weakened to a tropical depression as it passed over the Big Island in August 1991. Fefa's strong winds, heavy rains and flooding mainly assaulted the Big Island, but all of the Hawaiian Islands felt its effects.

As tropical storms and hurricanes made their presence known in the ocean waters surrounding the Hawaiian Islands, Kauai's prosperity also made a significant impact on the state's economic picture. Between the 1982 Hurricane Iwa and Hurricane Iniki in 1992, record numbers of visitors, a rapidly increasing population, low unemployment figures, and high volume real estate sales inundated Kauai.

By the end of the 1980s, the Hanalei Colony Resort, the Hanalei Bay Resort, the Waiohai and the Sheraton Kauai were filled to capacity more often than not, and condominiums and housing developments cropped up in Princeville and Poipu. In 1989, Kauai's visitor count reached an all-time high of 1,138,230. In the same year, the popular hotels and the new $60 million Waiohai were hosting a record visitor count of more than 1 million visitors.

All the hotels damaged by Hurricane Iwa had been repaired, yet the number and types of visitors continued on an upswing and caused a demand for more luxury accommodations. Kauai entered the "super luxury resort" arena when the Hyatt Regency Kauai and the Westin were constructed.

In the decade preceding Hurricane Iniki, tourism-related work provided the greatest number of employment opportunities, thereby forcing Kauai's former top ranking employer, the agricultural industry, into second place. From

1985, the unemployment steadily declined and reached an all-time low of 2.8 percent in 1989 at the height of Kauai's golden days.

The booming economy also gave rise to a significant increase in population. Between 1985 and the present, Kauai's population went from 44,400 to 55,700. With a boom in population to service the growing economy, residential projects experienced rapid development as well. The second phase of the Princeville expansion was underway, and major subdivision developments by principal landowners, including A&B and Amfac, were built.

Real estate sales also flourished. The highest number of real estate sales in Kauai's history occurred in 1987, with the largest dollar volume peaking at $193 million in 1990. The house party was short lived, however. By 1991, economic conditions caused the steepest decline in the real estate market since 1982.

With an infusion of international investors, predominantly Japanese honing in on the local real estate and resort development markets, land prices skyrocketed. Affordable housing became a crisis in the mid- to late-80s as home rental prices jumped from $500 per month to an average of $1,200 per month.

Kauai's economy had finally diversified with the advent of a cottage industry promoting products made on Kauai, and McBryde's (A&B) foray into large-scale coffee growing.

The early 1990s, however, brought forth the dark side of an international economy that was slipping into recession. A weakening Japanese economy caused Japanese investment interests in Hawaii to crumble. By the early part of 1992, Kauai's visitor industry showed signs of suffering due to the recent Persian Gulf war and the ensuing mainland U.S. recession. Tourism statistics prior to Hurricane Iniki for the period of 1991 and early 1992 dipped.

According to the statistics experts at First Hawaiian Bank's research department, Hurricane Iniki could not have hit at a worse time in the economic cycle. With the state entering one of the worst recessions in decades, incentives for many establishments quickly to restore ongoing operations did not exist.

The summer of 1992 was hot and dry. The trade winds often faltered, and the wiliwili trees' explosion of tangerine-colored blossoms mimicked the heat of the tropical sun.

While Hawaii's visitor industry lagged compared to previous seasons, Kauai was playing a starring role as the glamorous jungle backdrop for Steven Spielberg's movie Jurassic Park. Throngs of tourists hiked along the Na Pali coast, took helicopter rides, and languished on Kauai's white sand beaches. At summer's end, on September 5, the National Hurricane Center in Miami noted Tropical Depression 18-E. This system appeared to be a weak one that was dissipating to the southeast of Hawaii. But, on Sunday, September 6, it regenerated, strengthened and, as it moved west and north, developed into a tropical storm.

Tropical Depression (TD) 18-E, now west of 140 W longitude, was in the Central Pacific Hurricane Center's area of forecast responsibility. TD 18-E was christened Iniki, a Hawaiian word meaning "sharp, piercing wind." Between Thursday, September 10, and Friday, September 11, Iniki intensified and nearly equaled in force Hurricane Andrew, which had recently devastated parts of Florida. Iniki teetered and turned north, like an out-of-control top, toward Kauai and Oahu.

On Kauai, residents took notice of the approaching storm. On Thursday, September 10, they began to stockpile provisions, gas up their cars and batten down their homes and property. Residents were cautious and nervous.

The National Weather Service alerted Kauai's Civil Defense authorities that a hurricane watch would commence as of 5 p.m. Thursday. Within three hours, the watch was upgraded to a warning for Kauai, Niihau and Oahu.

At 5:30 a.m. on the morning of September 11, residents of Kauai and Oahu awoke to the eerie wails of Civil Defense warning sirens. Fear gripped the hearts of those

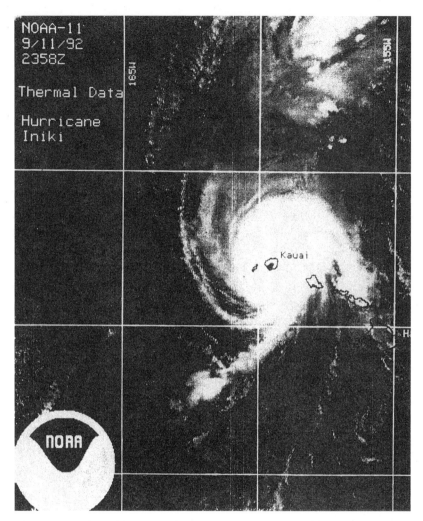

NOAA-11
9/11/92
2358Z

Thermal Data

Hurricane
Iniki

Kauai

NOAA

Figure 7.1 Satellite interpretation of thermal data associated with Hurricane Iniki over the island of Kauai. Courtesy of the National Weather Service.

who had witnessed Iwa's wrath ten years earlier. Excitement gripped those who had never experienced a hurricane. Confusion plagued visitors and transplants from landlocked mainland areas where "hurricane" was a foreign word. Many residents gathered up their most valuable and portable possessions, closed their homes and left for designated hurricane shelters. Others remained home, listening to the radio and trying to reassure their families, relatives and friends.

By 10 a.m. on September 11, the Honolulu International Airport was closed and guests of Waikiki's beachfront hotels had been evacuated. But, as forecasters followed the storm's path, it became increasingly evident that Iniki would brush Oahu and crash directly into Kauai.

By late afternoon, the eye of Iniki passed directly over Kauai (Figure 7.1). Recorded wind speeds ranged from 130 mph to 145 mph. An unverified gust recorded on an exposed northwest cliff at Makaha Ridge registered 227 mph.

The strongest, most terrifying hurricane ever to hit Hawaii, Iniki focused its wrath on Kauai and destroyed homes and businesses, flattened cane fields and shredded the island's lush vegetation. Little of the island remained unscathed following Iniki's rampage.

Sonny Gerardo, Kauai's Civil Defense Administrator, gave the following report:

"On the afternoon of September 10, Glenn Trapp, head of the Central Pacific Hurricane Center at the National Weather Service in Honolulu, informed me that a hurricane watch would be issued later that day. At 3 p.m. a briefing was given for the Civil Defense emergency staff, state district office heads, representatives of the Red Cross, and others involved in emergency management.

"Civil Defense staff members were instructed to go home and prepare their own homes for the storm. Nora Masuda, our secretary at Kauai Civil Defense headquarters, agreed to remain at headquarters while I went to prepare my home in Koloa. First, I drove to Poipu to observe the ocean. From Poipu Beach, the watery horizon looked 'hapai' (Hawaiian for pregnant), an indication of a massive storm surge. In decades past, Spouting Horn (an underwater cave that produces saltwater plumes when

waves pound into it) had been dredged by the Army Corps of Engineers to prevent its massive salt spray plumes from killing nearby sugar cane. Already, rockets of salt water were exploding thirty feet in the air.

"When I saw the storm surge battering Poipu's shoreline nearly twenty-four hours before Iniki was expected to hit land, I knew this hurricane was going to be a bad one. When I reached my home, there was a message from Glenn Trapp, head of the National Weather Service in Honolulu. I immediately returned his call. He said to me, 'Very bad news. . . the hurricane watch is being upgraded to a hurricane warning at 8:00 p.m.' I returned quickly to the Emergency Operating Center in the county building and reviewed my hurricane check list. At the EOC, the Volunteer Coordinator was busy making his calls and I asked him to coordinate the radio telecommunications system.

"Next, Joe Reed at the Oahu Civil Defense Office contacted me to discuss the sounding of the warning sirens. Both of us discussed the siren sounding for each county and determined the best time for sounding the warning sirens.

"Reed and I considered sounding the sirens during the night hours, however, we did not feel this was appropriate because many people might not hear it. So, Oahu officials calculated the time of the hurricane's arrival and scheduled the sounding for 5:30 a.m., on the morning of September 11. I decided to sound Kauai's sirens at the same time to minimize confusion. Since it was my decision, we planned to sound the sirens at 5:30 a.m., along with Oahu.

"After Mayor Yukimura returned to Kauai around midnight the night before Iniki struck, her administrative assistant Tom Batey briefed her about the *emergency situation. Although most decisions had been made before Yukimura's return from Hono- lulu, Batey was the person briefing her about the ongoing operations. I was not asked to be a part of this advisory process. However, by law and by emergency plans, the position of Civil Defense Agency Administrator is clearly to act as the first assistant to the Deputy Director of Civil Defense -- the Mayor--of each county in Hawaii.*

"At no time did the mayor ask me to brief her about the operations at the EOC. At this time, I was silently denied a decision-making role in the EOC. Yukimura took over control of Civil Defense opera- tions and made Batey her personal advisor. Clearly, my position of the Kauai Civil Defense Administra- tor was usurped and denied.

"The sounding of the sirens was almost can- celed entirely because Batey advised her that this was unnecessary. If acting Chief of Police Ken Robinson had not informed me about the attempted cancellation of the sirens, I wouldn't have known! It was after Robinson informed me that Yukimura and I argued the point about canceling the siren warn- ings. Mayor Yukimura changed her mind about the cancellation shortly after our discussion and we fi- nally sounded the sirens at 5:39 a.m., nine min- utes later than had been originally scheduled."

As the full impact of the hurricane blasted Kauai, the staff of KONG radio, Kauai's official Civil Defense station passed on all available information to the threatened popu- lace. Ed Kanoi, a popular local DJ, recounts his experience at the radio station.

"We're the Civil Defense station for this island. Unfortunately, we lost communications with Civil Defense very early. The radio antenna (that pro-

vides communication between Civil Defense officials and KONG radio) blew off the County Building. We were on the air until about four o'clock in the afternoon. I watched debris flying past the large window in the studio. Cars were shaking, wires were ripped off telephone poles, and then the poles themselves began to sway. Outside the office was an old metal container used as an icehouse. I saw it stand up on its side and then tumble down the road.

"Corrugated steel and iron rolled down the road like tissue paper. At 9:30 p.m., once the winds had decreased, we went outside to check our antenna. The 400-foot piece of steel was twisted like a pretzel. At that point, we scanned the radio dial to see if anybody was still on the air. All of Kauai's radio stations were out. We could pick up Honolulu stations, but they obviously had no idea how hard Kauai had been hit. They were reporting only Oahu concerns.

"At 1 a.m., we decided to see if we could get to Nawiliwili. It looked like a bombed out war zone. We went to the Coast Guard headquarters, but they'd lost all their radio equipment and had no communication with Honolulu. Next, we decided to go to the County Building because they have their own communication system with Oahu. There, I managed to talk with a ham radio operator on Oahu who hooked me up with a radio station. I did an interview for that station so they could relay the information back to Kauai. I knew with all the Kauai stations out of commission, our residents would be looking for Oahu stations."

The *Honolulu Advertiser* reported that "nearly every home between Haena and Kilauea sustained some damage; many had been destroyed." The scenery stretching beyond

105

Lumahai Beach toward the Na Pali Coast resembled the combined ravages of a forest fire and a ferocious windstorm. The usually green vegetation was stripped bare, twisted and mangled.

Kapaa High & Intermediate School Principal Wayne Watanabe recounted his experience at the high school, designated as a public shelter during the worst natural disaster in Kauai's history. The school provided shelter to more than 1,500 people.

"In the beginning, many tourists felt that this storm was a minor one. Mr. Youn (vice principal) and myself had to keep them in the rooms as they acted like true tourists--taking pictures of the wind, the sky, etc. As the wind escalated, they began to realize the seriousness of this hurricane alert.

"We utilized the cafeteria as our headquarters to coordinate the disaster plan. We, too, didn't realize the extent of the force of the hurricane. At one point, we were also 'clowning around' by taking pictures of each other. Suddenly, one part of the back wall caved in--blocks of wood about 4 feet by 15 feet started falling and we ran for our lives, outside in the storm. The wind was ferocious. Debris and remnants of our roof were swirling around us. We had to find shelter really fast. Finally, we found an open door to a restroom about 50 yards away from the cafeteria. I was never so terrified in my life.

"After what seemed an eternity, the wind decreased in velocity and we thought the storm was over. Therefore, I assigned our leadership group to assess the damage on our campus. Little did we know that the storm would reverse itself. The wind began to blow back to the ocean on its journey away from the island. I remember holding on for my dear life to a doorknob because all the rooms were locked.

Figure 7.2 Home near Wainiha Road, Haena, smashed by hurricane winds accelerating downslope from nearby mountains.

"Upon assessing the damages, it was reported to us that the gymnasium roof had caved in. Luckily, Kauai Fire Department personnel were in the gym and helped maintain order. They moved the people to another building. It was a miracle that only one person was hit on the head by falling debris. Before the storm, I remember instructing the people to pull the bleachers out to sit. They ended up hiding under them to shield themselves from the debris.

"As we began to set up communication lines, we tried to contact Civil Defense. We didn't have any flashlights. The bureaucracy of the Red Cross prevailed when we asked them for flashlights. They responded, 'You have to pick up a voucher!'"

Kapeka Chandler described the effects of Hurricane Iniki on her home in Haena.

"There were seventeen of us at home, ten adults

and seven children. We were all in the hallway and the front two bedrooms when the back two bedrooms went. Next, the roof flew off. Some roofing landed on our truck and busted the whole back. My son-in-law said, 'It's a good thing it hit the truck because that's probably the only thing insured.'"

The once quaint village of Hanalei lay in shambles. In Princeville, rows of condominiums sat exposed with their roofs cropped off. In Princeville alone, 279 homes were entirely destroyed their roofs, walls and contents scattered like matchsticks. Another 370 homes there received major damage.

In operation only one year since a multimillion dollar renovation, the Princeville Resort served as a shelter for many north shore residents. The resort continued to house homeless residents after the hurricane and fed people until the food ran out. Shelters in other areas of Kauai felt the crunch of caring for homeless people, too.

In the old sugar plantation town of Kilauea, Donna Schulze, age 68, and her husband George, age 70, tried to weather Iniki at their home, but at its height, they were forced to evacuate.

"During the hurricane, we huddled in a hallway with our cat, with supplies of candles, flashlights, blankets, and a change of clothing and water stacked around us. We listened to the radio. Then, we heard a terrible banging coming from the attic. The roof went off one end of the hallway and we heard empty luggage and the grandchildren's boogie boards flying against the walls. We pulled mattresses over our heads.

"I was so scared. There was nothing we could do. I've never felt so helpless. Two years ago, I was diagnosed with cancer and my husband had heart surgery. We held up pretty well. But this was differ-

Figure 7.3. Hurricane Iniki wreaked havoc on Kapaa. Above, debris blocks access to the Pono Fish Market.

ent. We had no control. At the height of the storm, the house was so full of water that we had to leave. With metal flying everywhere, we made it the two blocks to the Kilauea Neighborhood Center. But, there was so much scrap metal piled against the door, you couldn't open it. Then we saw that its roof was gone. Across the street was the little lava rock church. Fighting the wind, we made our way to it. We were invited in, and with twelve others, we spent the night."

Kapaa's main street looked like a war scene with collapsed buildings everywhere (Figure 7.3).

Respiratory therapist, Bill Glasscock, provided emergency care to hundreds of people at the Kapaa Armory.

"On Sunday, after the hurricane, people were asking the radio station to get help for children who had asthma. Because my respiratory equipment didn't need electrical power, I knew I could help. I went to my Kapaa office and loaded the equipment and oxygen cylinders into my truck and drove to the Armory. Major Daligdig, whose son was an asthma patient of mine, put me to work. Two medics from the Big Island and I were the only medical personnel at the armory.

"Initially, we treated serious cuts and slices from flying metal and glass. Within six hours, people heard that respiratory services were available and asthma cases started pouring in, one after the other. The military kept a log of my patient load. I treated 18 kids the first day, 20 the next, and then 30 a day for a week, all with severe respiratory difficulties.

"I was afraid my medicine and oxygen would run out. After two days they did. Then, the military supplied cylinders of oxygen, and medicine started arriving from drug companies. Three or four days later, another medical team arrived. We turned a section of the armory into a miniature hospital. I'd go in at seven in the morning, leave at seven or eight at night without taking a break.

"The military also flew me by helicopter to outlying communities to care for people with respiratory distress. I flew from Kapaa to the north shore, then across the center of the island to the west and south sides. What I saw was horrible. You couldn't distinguish which community was which. They all looked the same--just piles of trash. You'd be flying along over flattened sugar cane fields and toppled trees, and, all of sudden you'd see something that looked like a garbage dump. These were the remains of homes, littering the land. Kauai didn't look like Kauai anymore." (Figure 7.4)

Figure 7.4. Aerial photo of devestated community. Photographer Bill Howe.

Wailua, the ancient religious capital of Kauai, wasn't spared by Iniki, either.

From Wailua Homesteads, a trio of friends watched as their world blew apart. Donna Goodwin, an administrator, weathered the storm with her friends Pippa Smith, a social worker, and artist Clark Sealy. Her voice was choked with emotion as she told their hurricane story.

"Around noon, the winds picked up to about 40 mph. Excited, we went outside to look around. We even considered climbing Sleeping Giant Mountain, thinking we'd have time before the really heavy winds began. Instead, we decided to have lunch. We were sitting around the dining room table, with a red checkered tablecloth, when the lights went out at 1: 15 p.m. Later, we called it 'The Last Lunch.'"

"Listening to the radio, we heard that roofs were blowing off in Kalaheo. Our denial about the seriousness of the storm disintegrated. The DJ continued to report that winds were clocking up to 160 mph. I looked at Pippa and said, 'People are going to die in this storm.' Pippa, her face ashen, replied, 'We have to have a plan'. We gathered up mattresses and hauled them to a back room, which we thought would be the safest.

"Pippa's panic literally saved our lives. The dining room had a huge glass window archway near the ceiling. If we'd been sitting at the dining room table when it imploded, we'd have been shredded with flying glass. Huddled under mattresses, we heard an incredible, ear-splitting noise. After only the third or fourth really strong gust, the roof blew off. When things calmed down, I peeked out and saw sky. Not only the roof was missing, but also the whole front of the house was gone. We were all barefoot so we began to look for shoes."

§§§§§

The fury of the wind and its devastation on land equaled the devastation wrought by stormy seas. Sixty boats were damaged or lost, and all four of Kauai's boat harbors were mangled.

At Nawiliwili Harbor, the storm surge tossed and stacked yachts on top of each other like children's toys. Cultural anthropologists and researchers David Lewis and his wife, Dr. Mimi George stayed aboard their 32-foot sail boat, the Gryphon, which was moored in the harbor. The following entry is from their ship's log.

"At 3:30 p.m., wind is well over 100 knots. Beneteau 34 in next slip parted its starboard bow

warp and mounted our deck, demolishing gallows, stanchions and bulwarks, all with enormous shocks. Mimi futility tried to secure her, wearing safety harness. The Beneteau next took out a chain plate and smashed our solid 8" diameter spruce mast at the deck, broke boom, gaff and fife rail and at last came free to drift ashore to leeward. Meanwhile, the Columbia 20, on our other side, came briefly aboard, was holed on the dock and sank alongside."

At the time of Iniki, Iwa Batalona had been working for Dollar Rent-A-Car at Lihue airport for ten years.

"I arrived at the airport about 5:30 a.m., the same time the sirens went off. We soon heard that people were being told to get to the shelters by 10:30. But flights were still coming in and people were still renting cars. What were we going to do with the tourists? We told them to catch busses to the shelter at the War Memorial Convention Center in Lihue. A lot of tourists arrived with no idea a hurricane was going to hit us. I couldn't believe that the airlines flew people in that day, knowing a hurricane was coming. When the hurricane hit, there were 1,100 rental cars in Dollar's fleet and most of them were rented. When the tourists finally left Kauai, Dollar had to search all over the island to find these cars. Wherever Dollar employees lived, they'd search their area and write down license plate numbers. Then, the company would make a field sweep."

Besides severe damage to most of Poipu's hotels, many private homes in the once beautiful south shore community were simply gone, masticated by the sea or crumpled and transplanted far inland (Figure 7.5). One house that had been transported well above the beachfront road sported a black spray-painted sign that read, "Compliments of Iniki Movers."

Figure 7.5 Kauai's tourist mecca, Poipu, in tatters, both physically and economically. Photo by Bill Howe

Along Hoone Road, the devastation was particularly ferocious (Figure 7.6). Julie and Rick Haviland, owners of a Poipu water-sports business, lived along this shoreline road in a small house.

"We didn't know if our house would survive the hurricane. Not having any insurance, we put everything of value in our van. We didn't know where to go. By morning, the waves and surf were so big and so loud, you could hardly hear the warning sirens.

"At about 11 :30 a.m., we decided to take a drive around Poipu, although the police had already blocked off many roads. When we arrived at our shop, just above the intersection of Lawai and Poipu Roads, our business neighbor, Ed Sills, was boarding up the windows. He said, 'This building is solid as a rock. Stay here.'

"From the back of our store, I could see waves

Figure 7.6. Oceanfront Poipu home wrecked beyond recognition.

---

crashing over the roofs of houses on Poipu Beach. The waves sucked back and broke far out, propelling tons and tons of white water onto the shore. You could see waves billowing up into steam above a white sea. What it was like down there in the houses was too frightening to think about.

"My heart sank. Watching the waves, I thought, 'What a joke that I put all my little girl's books in a plastic bag and stuck them in the attic.' I thought about all the other stuff I stuck up there, including Christmas presents I'd purchased early. I knew my neighborhood wouldn't be intact when the waves receded. Then the rain came and you couldn't see the ocean any longer.

"After the storm, Rick and I went down to our neighborhood, not expecting to see anything standing. The good news was we still had a house. The bad news was that hardly anyone else did."

Figure 7. 7 A westside home ripped to shreds.

Further west, more communities succumbed to Iniki's destructive path. Buildings along Hanapepe's historic main street--that once reflected the town's prosperity as one of the largest rice-producing districts in the territory of Hawaii--were reduced to rubble. A westside landmark, the Seto Market, was virtually unrecognizable.

From their modest and comfortable home in Hanapepe Heights, Dave and Janet Leopold endured Iniki. Janet, who works for the National Botanical Tropical Gardens in Lawai and her husband, who is a registered nurse at Kauai Veterans Memorial Hospital in Waimea, did not fathom the danger of staying at home during the storm.

"When the lattice in the carport exploded, we decided to go inside the house. We went into the living room and sat on the couch and watched our neighbors' roof flapping, and then it just lifted off. As we were sitting there, we heard a huge crash and

that's when somebody's roof rafters came right through the ceiling, only a few feet away from where we were sitting.

"We decided it was time to crawl under our big dining room table. We dragged mattresses from the bedroom to put around the sides of the table."

Iniki slammed through Waimea at wind speeds of 130 to 160 mph (Figure 7.7). Ako Store was ravaged, the Waimea High School gym lost its roof, and the Hawaiian Language Church was torn into several large chunks and strewn across the churchyard.

Landis Ignacio was Kekaha Sugar Company's agriculture operations manager at the time.

"We were in my wife's home, a wooden structure, in Waimea Valley. Looking outside, we could see everything flying--the neighbors' roofs, an entire garage, tool sheds, trees--just falling all over the place. I had my chair back against the wall and the wall was actually bowing in. It pushed me into the room and I realized that this was a very serious matter. I was physically scared. I had my wife and my daughter barricaded in a closet with a mattress over them.

"The next morning I needed to get back to Kekaha to see what I could do, realizing that we needed to get the roadways cleared for emergencies. And, people in the shelters wanted to go home as soon as possible, but the roads were very dangerous. So we started clearing the roads.

"There was no way to drive a car out of Waimea Valley. The roads were completely blocked or washed out and power lines were down, so I walked out. I came across a friend who had a truck and he was on his way home, so he gave me his truck. It took over an hour and a half to get just the three

miles to Kekaha!"

Westsider Marilyn Planas was the assistant director of nursing at Kauai Veterans Memorial Hospital in Waimea. During Iniki, the hospital doubled as a hurricane shelter.

"Just after the sirens went off at 5:30 a.m., I received a call from the hospital to come in right away for a department heads meeting. I packed an extra pair of uniforms because I knew once I got to the hospital, I'd be there for a couple of days. It never crossed my mind when I left my house to take one last look around because I may never see it the same way again. The only thought on my mind was, 'get to work, get to work!'

"When I got to KVMH I heard how bad the approaching hurricane was. At the 7 a.m. meeting, they said the storm had sustained winds of about 140 mph. I remembered Iwa, which was 80 or 90 mph.

"Community people were wall to wall in the hospital because the shelters were overloaded. I estimated roughly 400 local residents and a patient load of about 25, including the ICU. In addition to people, we had nonhuman evacuees too. There were dogs barking, cats meowing, birds chirping in the hospital! I couldn't get used to those sounds. I never heard a dog bark in a hospital and my first reaction was, that animal does NOT belong in here! But we confined the people who brought their pets to the outpatient area so it wasn't any kind of a threat to the sick patients.

"We lost electricity about noon, then we were on emergency power. We had prepared for the loss of the water supply by filling up basins and containers. The military had brought in a large water tanker for us before the storm and this we used for flush-

Figure 7.8 The son of photographer Jim Denny stands on one of many boulders that washed over Kekaha's Route 50 again in 1992.

ing toilets and washing. The dietary department prepared lots of food for patients, staff and people who came in.

"The nurses had all their patients evacuated from their rooms into the hallways by 1 o'clock. By 2 p.m. the force of the wind started breaking the windows in patients' rooms. The worst was between 3 and 4 o'clock. There were leaks all over the place."

At Kekaha, some pavement chunks of Kaumualii Highway went surfing into oceanfront yards. Large rocks, sand and coral adorned the remainder of the highway. Once again, as in previous hurricanes, Route 50 became part of Kekaha Beach (Figure 7.8).

John Tenuto of Kekaha, a meteorological technician for the Pacific Missile Range Facility, finished work at the base and headed to his Kekaha home.

"Since we are not in the weather forecasting business here at PMRF, I delivered the info I received from the National Weather Service and the Navy Weather Station at Pearl Harbor. As I was plotting the storm, I discovered that the info seemed like it was several hours behind.

"Iniki was initially predicted to arrive between 5 and 7 p.m., but when I left the base at 11 a.m., Iniki was only 130 miles south of Lihue. I wanted to leave and get back to Kekaha to be with my family. I decided to hand carry the chart of the storm's position to Navy Housing where Commanding Officer Captain Robert Mullins was one of the last people exiting the area. We met on the road and I handed him the position, which I told him to advance by a couple of hours.

"When I reached Kekaha, the wind was about 35-40 knots. I made it home by avoiding Route 50, where the waves were already demolishing the highway.

"Fortunately for Kauai, the storm picked up speed as it was traveling through here. Had it been slower and given us another hour of that intensified wind, I don't think that there would have been any building left standing on the entire island."

Every community on Kauai suffered losses from Hurricane Iniki. Residents questioned themselves about why nearly every church on the island lost its steeple, roof, walls, or was totally destroyed. With their confidence in their physical safety shaken, posttraumatic stress syndrome was a common experience.

Hurricane Iniki was granted the status of the worst hurricane of the century to affect the Fiftieth State. Iniki's fury was so far-reaching that not only did it affect Kauai, the storm caused significant damage on Oahu, Maui and the Big Island, as well.

Iniki was the worst natural disaster ever to hit Hawaii and the most severe hurricane in a hundred years. Iniki's overall damages were estimated at $2.2 billion, only $77 million of which was accounted for by Oahu.

According to FEMA's final damage assessment of Kauai's 20,000 homes, 11,700 were damaged; 1,200 were totally destroyed; 3,000 suffered severe damage; and 7,500 acquired minor damage. More than 7,000 people were left homeless.

Most of Kauai's 70 hotels and condominiums were severely damaged, destroying the visitor industry, which had been the principal economic base of the island. Because Kauai's main form of income depended on the tourism trade, Hurricane Iniki dealt a severe blow to the island's economy, which has still not completely recovered. Major damage to 7,200 hotel and condo units has caused millions of dollars in lost revenues from the tourism industry.

Kauai, the third most visited Hawaiian Island after Oahu and Maui, greeted one million visitors annually prior to Iniki. As of July 1993, only four of the island's major hotels, including the Hyatt Regency Kauai, Sheraton Princeville Resort, the Outrigger, and Kauai Beach Resort, were reopened. It wasn't until May of 1994 that the Westin--formerly Kauai's largest employer with more than 1,000 people on the payroll and the largest property tax payer--was purchased by the Marriott chain. The transformed resort officially reopened in July 1995, with roughly 250 new employees. As of 2001, Coco Palms is still closed and the Waiohai is being demolished and rebuilt.

Agriculture on Kauai suffered $78 million worth of damages due to Hurricane Iniki. The greatest impact of Iniki on Kauai's agriculture was seen in the already troubled sugar industry. Approximately 70 percent of the crop had been harvested before the hurricane, but effects on production continued for years.

A macadamia nut orchard was virtually flattened and no plans to replant those trees materialized. Only about half of the 1992 coffee crop could be salvaged. The flower and nursery industry suffered similarly.

One resident said, "It was painful, but not surprising, to witness manmade structures fallen, but almost harder was seeing fallen Macadamia nut trees dotting the island's hillsides, like herds of slaughtered buffalo."

Lifelines

Kauai's entire power grid fell due to Iniki. Compared to Hurricane Iwa, the disruption of electrical and communications systems was longer and more severe. By the end of November, more than two months after Iniki, ten percent of Kauai's residents still didn't have telephone or electrical service.

For safety reasons, Kauai Electric discontinued commercial power at 1:20 p.m. on the day of the hurricane. Of the island's 1,700 transmission poles, the winds felled 450, along with five transmission towers; 5,550 (of 15,000) distribution poles; and 280 (of 800) miles of distribution wires.

Kauai county formed an Electrical Power Council, a collaboration between private, state, federal, military and county agencies. The council met daily to prioritize the resumption of power necessary for critical services and facilities, including water distribution, sewage treatment and power to medical facilities and fire stations.

The military assisted with transporting utility poles, cables and personnel. Work crews from affiliate power companies on the mainland deluged Kauai to assist in power restoration. The Army installed generators in critical facilities.

Hurricane Iniki knocked out all telephone communications. Both of the two microwave towers that carry long distance telephone service were felled. Limited interisland calling, for emergency uses only, resumed on September 16 when GTE Hawaiian Tel received new tower dishes. Each fire station received a working phone. GTE established phone banks around the island where disaster victims could make free,

Figure 7.9 A child's teddy bear lies ontop of a heap of rubble that once was someone's home.

three-minute long distance calls. The island's cellular telephone system was quickly repaired and came into widespread use.

All island radio stations were incapacitated. KONG radio, the Civil Defense station, didn't resume transmission until Sunday morning, September 13. For the intensity of Hurricane Iniki and all the loss associated with it, there was little loss of life (Figure 7.9). Two Iniki-related deaths were reported on Kauai and one on Oahu. According the National Weather Service, limited loss of life was due to ample warning, an excellent response by Civil Defense and the public, evacuation of all coastal areas, and the level of awareness created by recent press coverage of Hurricane Andrew.

Predisposing Weather Conditions

According to the National Weather Service's lead forecaster Hans Rosendal, Iniki, a small but intense hurricane, was classified as a minimal Category Four on the Saffir-Simpson Scale.

"As it approached Kauai, winds averaged 145 mph with gusts to 175 mph, with a central pressure of 938 millibars. When Iniki passed over the island, the winds decreased slightly to 130 mph, with gusts to 160 mph, and the central pressure increased to 945 millibars.

"Iniki formed about 1,450 nautical miles southwest of Baja, California. By September 9, the storm had continued to strengthen and reached a point 385 miles south southwest of Hilo on the Big Island. Up to this point, the storm was similar to other typical hurricanes, which move to the south of the Hawaiian Islands.

"As Iniki continued west northwestward, conditions formed that turned Iniki northward on a collision course with Kauai. The airflow pattern in the western Pacific changed. A series of short wave troughs dug a long wave trough southward along the International Dateline. The subtropical ridge, which held Iniki in check, weakened. When a southwesterly flow developed to the east of the trough, it appeared Iniki might take a more northward track.

"On the morning of September 10, Iniki was 420 miles south southwest of Honolulu and moving west. By 5 p.m., it began turning to the northwest. During the evening hours of September 10, Iniki slowly turned northward, propelled by a southwesterly flow ahead of a cold trough and a low situated to the northwest. Turning north, Iniki accelerated."

The El Niño affects the occurrence of hurricanes in Hawaii. In the area where Iniki formed, water temperatures remained one to three degrees Centigrade warmer than normal. Scientists later agreed that El Niño was still in effect at the time of Iniki's inception. Many of the circulation peculiarities associated with

El Niño, such as dry winters in Hawaii and floods in California, existed, Rosendal explained.

"Iniki may have been a product of El Niño or of the dispersing warm waters from the equator. An atypical late season hurricane, it formed farther west and south. Hurricanes traveling on their way west northwestward from the waters off southern Mexico move over progressively cooler waters. By the time the storms reach 140 W longitude, 1,000 miles east of the Big Island, a cooler, drier, more stable environment usually causes them to weaken. Hurricanes that develop farther west and remain on a more southerly track, like Iniki, are more likely to reach Hawaiian waters."

Regardless of why Iniki struck Kauai, the fact remained that this hurricane would have far-reaching implications. Unemployment figures one month after Iniki reached 25%, and moving companies and speculators believed that nearly 7,000 people left the island due to the debilitated economy and lack of housing.

The industry hardest hit was that of tourism. Major damage to 7,200 hotel and condo units and damage to public parks and recreational facilities caused millions of dollars in lost revenues from the tourism industry. During the ten-year period following Iniki, islanders began to realize that alternative forms of business, besides tourism, needed to be established.

§§§§§

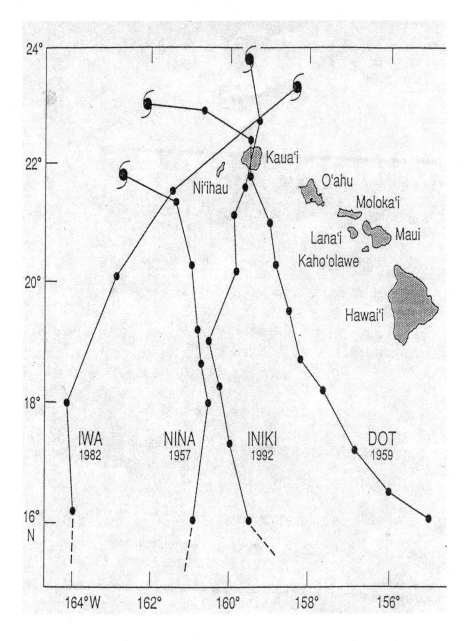

Figure 8.1 Tracks of the four most important hurricanes in Hawaii since 1950. These tracks are limited to the vicinity of the Hawaiian Islands. Source: Schroeder.

Chapter Eight

The Next Hurricane

Most weather forecasters and Civil Defense officials, when referring to the "next hurricane," don't ask if there will be another hurricane. Instead, they ask when the next hurricane will strike.

This philosophy is intended to ensure the safety of islanders and visitors by making them aware of the possibility of the next hurricane and the need for being prepared.

Hardly anyone expected a hurricane as powerful as Iniki to strike Hawaii. The threat to the Hawaiian Islands from hurricanes remains real, so it is everyone's responsibility to be prepared and to know what actions to take if a hurricane threatens.

The National Weather Service Warning System

The National Weather Service is responsible for warning Civil Defense officials, news agencies, and the public about approaching storms. This is accomplished through the reporting of designated National Weather Service centers in both the Pacific and Atlantic.

The National Hurricane Center located near Miami, Florida, is responsible for hurricane forecasting for the Atlantic Basin, which encompasses the Caribbean Sea and the Gulf of Mexico, and for the North Pacific east of 140 west longitude. This area of the Pacific includes the area southwest of Mexico where most eastern North Pacific tropical hurricanes develop and die.

The Central Pacific Hurricane Center (CPHC) is co-located with the Honolulu Weather Forecast Office. The CPHC issues all tropical cyclone warnings, watches, advisories, discussions, and statements for tropical cyclones in the Central Pacific from 140 degrees west longitude to the International Dateline. The Weather Forecast Office in Honolulu forecasts programs for public, aviation and marine interests in Hawaii. Aviation responsibilities extend into the north Central Pacific, while marine responsibilities cover the central North and South Pacific.

The Joint Typhoon Warning Center, located in Hawaii, is responsible for the western North Pacific west of the International Dateline. This area is the most active tropical cyclone region in the world. The U.S. Navy in cooperation with the U.S. Air Force operates the Joint Typhoon Warning Center.

The National Weather Service is a line component of the National Oceanic and Atmospheric Administration (NOAA) for specialized marine and aviation advisories. When the National Hurricane Center, the Central Pacific Hurricane Center or the Joint Typhoon Warning Center issue advisories for the public, marine and aviation interests, the National Weather Service office conveys the information and issues local statements for their areas of warning responsibility.

The National Weather Service has been well utilized over the years since the launch of the first TIROS satellite, and its staff has learned to cope with many emergencies.

The Honolulu National Weather Service Office and Central Pacific Hurricane Center have standby emergency power and contingency plans in the event of commercial power failures.

In the past decade, this backup plan was put to the test. During a one-month period in 1992, all three U.S.-operated hurricane centers were in or near the path of hurricanes. The National Hurricane Center in Miami, Florida was blasted by Hurricane Andrew; the Joint Typhoon Warning Center in Guam was hit by Typhoon Omar; and the Central Pacific Hurricane Center in Honolulu felt the peripheral effects of Hurricane Iniki. Each center, however, was able to continue its hurricane surveillance independently or through collaborative efforts with other centers.

Civil Defense Response

Civil Defense networks are located throughout the U.S. They were created by the federal government through the Federal Emergency Management Agency (FEMA) to help residents cope with severe conditions before, during, and after a disaster. Each county in Hawaii has a Civil Defense agency. On Kauai, FEMA and the County of Kauai fund the agency.

After the National Weather Service issues hurricane warnings, state and county Civil Defense agencies convey those warnings to the public. Civil Air Patrol pilots assist local Civil defense agencies by monitoring and reporting developing systems. Local police officers and firefighters in emergency vehicles man roving patrols. These vehicles are equipped with sirens and public address units, allowing the teams to directly alert residents in threatened areas.

Each county in Hawaii also has audio warning systems consisting of outdoor siren units and indoor siren simulator monitors. Positioned in multiple strategic areas of each island, the outdoor sirens alert various communities to impending danger. This system is tested on the first working day of every month at 11:45 a.m., so that the public is familiar with the sound made by the sirens and so that officials can make sure that the system is functioning properly. Similar indoor siren systems have been installed in hotels, hospitals, schools, and other facilities where large numbers of people congregate.

When a natural disaster is imminent, both types of sirens sound a steady three-minute tone, which signals an emergency situation. The three-minute steady tone is followed by a one-minute silence. This pattern is repeated each hour for three cycles.

Civil Defense officials also contact the island or area's

designated Emergency Broadcast Radio Station to broadcast the reason for the siren sounding. Other radio stations monitor the Emergency Broadcast Station and also broadcast the information.

In the Hawaiian Islands, as elsewhere, the National Weather Service officials rely on Civil Defense personnel to coordinate and carry out evacuation plans in a hurricane emergency. People living or vacationing in low lying, flood-prone areas or those who are housed in poorly constructed buildings are encouraged to leave for designated shelters. Shelters are usually opened in school gymnasiums or large, public auditoriums. In high-rise buildings, such as Waikiki hotels, guests are urged to practice "vertical evacuation," by moving to floors above ground level.

During emergencies, National Weather Service meteorologists stay in constant contact with Civil Defense officials and advise them of changes in the storm situation.

Role of the Military

Federal, state and local responses to a hurricane are designed to begin before the storm impacts land. As the hurricane approaches, counties that may be affected are placed on a state of emergency alert. Emergency operation centers are activated, and emergency plans are initiated. Hawaii National Guard troops are placed on standby alert.

When the hurricane subsides, U.S. military support is activated as soon as the Presidential Disaster Declaration is signed. This triggers FEMA to create the Joint Task Force. The Joint Task Force includes military personnel from the Army, Marines, Navy, Air Force, Coast Guard, Hawaii Air National Guard, and Hawaii Army National Guard. In the wake of the disaster, military response efforts include the provision of generators, water, food, shelter, and construction materials. The military also provides health and medical assistance, cargo airlifts and passenger transportation (Figure 8.2 and 8.3). Troops sweep large areas for emergency debris removal and transport.

Figure 8.2 Pearl Harbor September 12, 1992. Troops of the 25th Infantry boarding the USS Belleau Wood were deployed to aid in disaster relief efforts in the aftermath of Iniki. Photos courtesy of Pacific Missile Range Facility by Bill Howe.

Figure 8.3. Pearl Harbor, September 30, 1992. Military vehicles line up to board the USS Belleau Wood. The transportation of troops and equipment to Kauai was part of Task Force Garden Isle, a joint military disaster relief effort.

After the governor proclaims the state a major disaster area, the state's Major Disaster Fund can be tapped to provide emergency relief funds, food stamps, relocation expenses, housing loans, and other temporary financial support.

The collaboration of the National Weather Service, local Civil Defense agencies and the military have made living in Hawaii safer. Because of recent direct-hit experiences especially during Iwa and Iniki, and overwhelming evidence that many other potentially damaging storms skirt the Hawaiian Islands on a regular basis, scientists and officials have developed and instituted comprehensive plans that lessen property damage and save countless lives.

§§§§§

Advancements in the Warning System

Today, emerging weather patterns around the globe are recorded by satellites in outer space and studied by National Weather Service meteorologists back on earth. The future now holds even greater promise to improve the hurricane warning capability of the National Weather Service. The National Weather Service is currently undergoing a modernization program, which will employ the newest technology and the latest scientific advances. This will lead to better hurricane forecasting and more effective warnings.

Major improvements in longer-range hurricane forecasts (36-72 hours) will come through better quality and quantity of observations and improved dynamic models. Global, hemispheric and regional models show considerable promise.

The Department of Transportation's Federal Aviation Administration and the Department of Defense join the National Weather Service in acquiring these new technologies. The geographical placement of the new radars and automated surface observing systems is coordinated by the three agen cies, thereby providing more uniform coverage.

Automated surface observations systems (ASOS) will relieve personnel from the manual collection of surface observations. This sophisticated system will provide data on pressure, temperature, wind direction and speed, visibility, cloud ceiling heights, and type and intensity of precipitation on a nearly continuous basis. As many as 1,000 ASOS sites function in the U.S. under the auspices of the Federal Aviation Administration and the National Weather Service. The Department of Defense is also considering the acquisition of additional units. The observational data provided by the ASOS system supports aviation operations and provides meteorological data needed by severe weather, flash flood, and river flood forecasting programs. The capability to observe and transmit critical changing weather conditions almost as they occur represents an important enhancement for improving warning and forecast services.

The next series of Geostationary Operational Environmental Satellites (GOES) are expected to provide higher resolution sounding data and be more accurate than the information currently being received from GOES satellites.

Polar orbit satellite systems are also being upgraded. For longer-range forecasting, soundings from the polar orbiting satellites provide enhanced numerical forecast models. The Advanced Microwave Sounding Unit, to be flown on the NOAA K-M satellite series, will provide global soundings in cloudy regions at about the same level of accuracy as those presently produced in cloud-free areas. These new satellites will complement the latest radars and automated surface observing systems. The information provided by these systems will be shared by participating agencies.

Utilizing Doppler radar technology, Next Generation Weather Radars (NEXRAD) will add new dimensions to hurricane warning capabilities by providing much needed information on tropical cyclone wind fields and their changes as they move inland. Local offices will be able to provide more accurate short-term warnings as rain bands, high winds and possible tornadoes move toward specific locations.

By calculating the speed and direction of motion of developing weather disturbances, NEXRAD will provide more accuracy and timeliness of NWS warning services. The NWS plans to operate 121 NEXRAD systems; the remainder of the NEXRAD systems will be located at Federal Aviation Administration and Department of Defense locations.

National Oceanic and Atmospheric Administration NOAA Weather Radio broadcasts National Weather Service warnings, watches, forecasts and other hazard information 24 hours a day. NOAA furnishes this public service, which is under the auspices of the Department of Commerce. The NOAA Weather Radio network has more than 425 stations in the 50 states and near adjacent coastal waters, Puerto Rico, the U.S. Virgin Islands, and U.S. Pacific Territories. The network is constantly upgrading its technology to provide the best weather reporting service possible.

Additional NOAA Weather Radio transmitters will continue to expand the nationwide network coverage to more rural areas and with more hazard-specific information to a particular listening area. Digital technology has provided automated broadcasts for quicker service, and it enhances information used for broadcast, cable, satellites and other media through the Federal Communications Commission's Emergency Alert System.

NOAA weather receivers should be standard equipment in every home and be placed in hospitals, schools, churches, nursing homes, restaurants, grocery stores, recreation centers, office buildings, sports facilities, theaters, retail stores, bus and train stations, airports, marinas, and other public gathering places.

Preparedness

For schools, businesses and the home, preparedness begins with a plan of action. This plan should be kept up to date and practiced frequently. Numerous public service messages, brochures and other material aimed at hurricane pre-

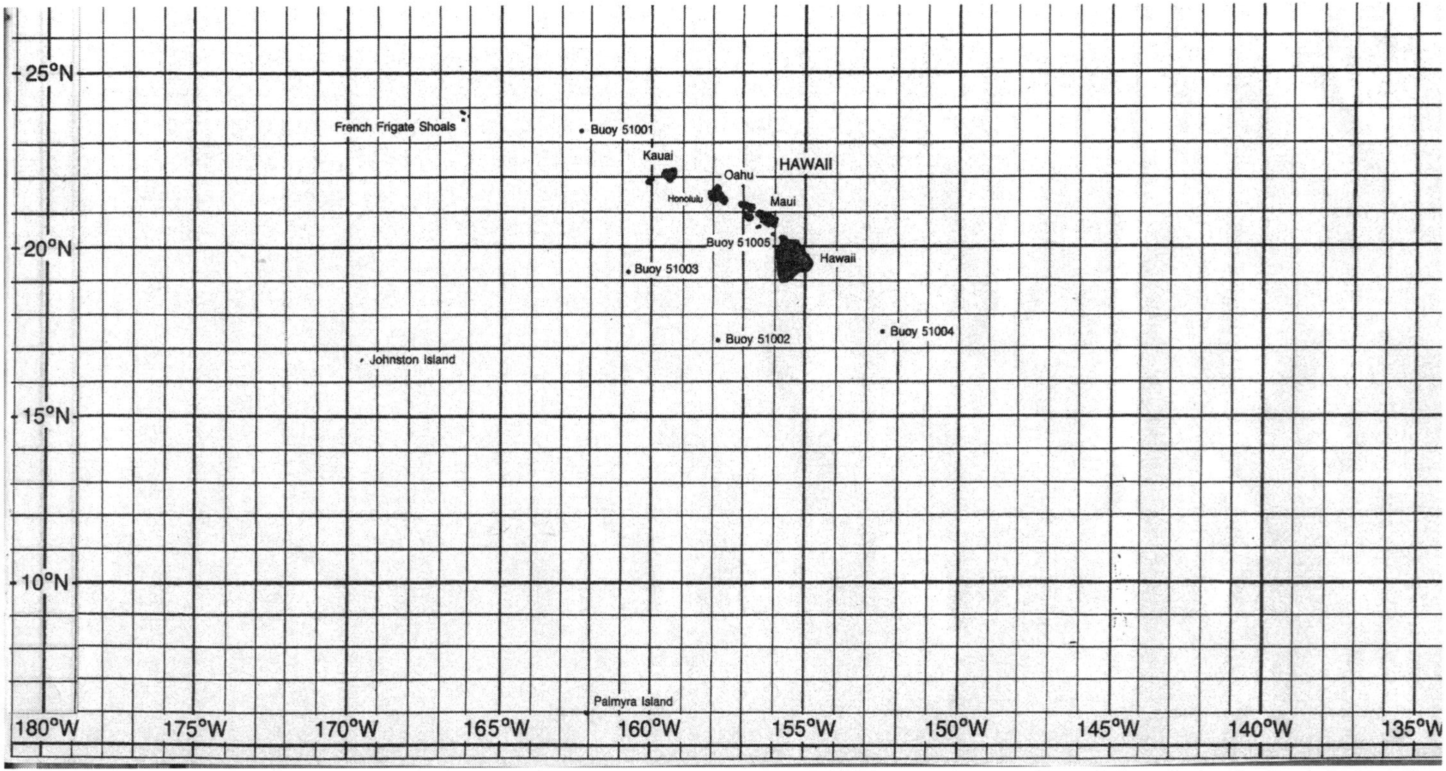

Figure 8.4 Sample hurricane tracking map. When listening to NOAA weather radio advisories, place a dot at the intersecting coordinates according to reports of the longitude and latitude. Contine to place dots at these coordinates as they are reported (every six hours or more), then draw a line between each dot to chart the hurricane or storm's progress and direction. Source: National Weather Service.

paredness are available through local government agencies, in local newspapers, and at the American Red Cross head-quarters in your area.

Long-term Planning

Safer and stronger building practices are essential for the future. Emergency management teams can provide safety programs, but it is up to individuals and businesses to cooperate and make specific preparations for their own safety and the integrity of their homes and property.

Checking with your county's Building Department for recommendations on fortifying your home or building against hurricane winds is strongly advised. Many homes and buildings in Hawaii have been constructed without the proper permits or inspections. Because these structures are built without even the minimum hurricane requirements, they may damage properly built structures and endanger lives.

Safe building practices include creating a complete load path with ties from the roof to the foundation and the use of hurricane clips and straps. Nailing down roof sheathing is critical and should include the right size nails, proper spacing of nails and nails that won't corrode.

Windows and sliding glass doors can cause a building to implode or explode. Besides proper installation and the use of glass that meets safety standards, the use of storm shutters or nailing plywood across glass surfaces should be standard practice for every home.

It is each person's responsibility to tie down, store or remove items that can become wind-borne debris. Tie downs are recommended for any temporary buildings and buildings on piers or concrete slabs.

Pressure-treated lumber and corrosion-resistant fasteners will aid against insect infestation and weathering. Periodic inspection and maintenance are sensible ways to protect a home.

Residents should be aware of the flood history of their specific area. Those living in areas vulnerable to storm surge and flooding from rivers or excessive rain should be aware of specific routes inland that can lead them safely to shelters or other public buildings. Helpful examples of coastal areas prone to flooding can be found in the front of your local telephone book.

Every family and individual living in the Hawaiian Islands is advised to stock up on at least two weeks worth of nonperishable food, bottled water, and prescriptions at the beginning of each hurricane season. Make or buy a first aid kit and replenish it as necessary.

Useful supplies you may wish to purchase ahead of time include basic camping gear (tent, camp stove and fuel, propane lantern, tarps, and mosquito repellant), a generator, a gas grill, a chain saw, and a portable toilet.

Prior to hurricane season, review the working condition of emergency equipment, such as flashlights and battery-powered radios. Have a supply of plastic containers with lids for storing valuables and important documents.

In the yard, keep trees and shrubbery trimmed. Cut weak branches and trees that could fall or bump against the house. Any loose objects in the yard can potentially be lethal weapons in hurricane winds. Don't wait until the last moment to minimize items in the yard, garage or around the house, and have a plan for storing these items if a hurricane threatens. If you own a boat, decide well ahead of time where to move or store it.

Review your insurance policy to ensure it provides adequate coverage. Elderly individuals and those with special needs should contact their local office of emergency management for assistance. Contact your local National Weather Service office, emergency management office, or American Red Cross chapter for additional information.

Advisories

When a tropical hurricane threatens land, **watches** and **warning**s are issued for people living in areas that may be affected. Normally, the National Weather Service issues public advisories every six hours. When storms approach or other major weather changes are anticipated, intermediate advisories and local statements are issued to the public. Weather Service personnel use information from Doppler radar, storm spotters, satellites, and other sources to issue bulletins, which are broadcast over local NOAA Weather Radio stations and retransmitted by many local radio and television stations. With this information, local emergency management and public safety officials can activate local warning systems to alert communities of an impending threat.

The Hurricane Watch

When a hurricane watch is broadcast, this indicates the possibility that hurricane conditions could develop within 36 hours or less. A watch is sometimes announced when a tropical storm which is expected to intensify to hurricane strength approaches. The hurricane watch may also be issued for fringing vicinities surrounding a hurricane warning area.

If a hurricane watch is announced, closely monitor radio, TV, NOAA Weather Radio, or hurricane hotline telephone numbers for official bulletins. Follow instructions issued by local officials. Complete preparation activities, such as putting up storm shutters and storing or tying down loose objects. Get your hurricane supplies and first aid kits in order and ready for use.

The Hurricane Warning

A hurricane warning is issued when severe weather is imminent or occurring. The warning indicates a high probability that hurricane conditions will develop over an area within 24 hours or less. Although it is not certain that hurricane conditions will occur, residents are urged to make all necessary preparations.

Again, monitor radio, TV and NOAA Weather Radio. Fuel and service family vehicles. Cover all windows and door openings with shutters or other shielding materials. Install batteries in radios and flashlights. Store outdoor lawn furni-

138

ture and other loose, lightweight objects, such as garbage cans, garden tools, potted plants, and sports equipment. Check and replenish first aid supplies. Have on hand an extra supply of cash.

Evacuation

As previously mentioned, a network of indoor and outdoor warning sirens will sound when there is immediate danger of a hurricane. Evacuation, at this point, is a personal choice, unless mandated by civil defense officials, firefighters or the police. With new building codes in place following Hurricane Iniki, Civil Defense officials hope that the need for residents to evacuate to public shelters is lessened.

If you live in a mobile home, DO NOT stay in it under any circumstances. They are unsafe in high wind and/or hurricane conditions, no matter how well they are fastened to the ground. Evacuate if you live in an area of potential flooding and leave early (if possible, in daylight). Notify family members or friends who live outside of the storm's vicinity of your evacuation plans.

Leave early to avoid heavy traffic, roads blocked by early floodwaters, and bridges impassable due to high winds. Put food and water out for a pet if you cannot take it with you. (Public shelters and most hotels or motels do not allow pets).

Hurricane shelters are available. Check with your county's Civil Defense office or American Red Cross for the shelter location nearest you. If you evacuate to a shelter bring a first aid kit, medicine, baby food and diapers, cards, games, books, toiletries, battery-powered radio, flashlight with extra batteries, blankets or sleeping bags, identification, valuable papers (particularly insurance policies), and cash.

Do not return home until officials announce that your area is safe. Proof of residency may be required in order to re-enter evacuation areas. If your home or building has structural damage, do not enter until officials check it.

Staying Home

If officials have not ordered evacuation in your area, and you feel the house or building you are in is safe to weather the storm, stay at home. Tape and board up windows. Fill sterilized jugs and bottles with drinking water. Fill the bathtub, the washing machine and any kind of large containers with water for sanitary purposes. Turn the refrigerator to the maximum cold setting and open it only when necessary. Turn off utilities if told to do so by authorities. Turn off propane tanks and unplug small appliances.

During the height of the storm, stay away from windows and doors even if they are covered. Take refuge in a small interior room, closet, or hallway and bring a battery-powered radio and a flashlight with you. Close all interior doors. Secure and brace external doors, particularly double inward-opening doors and garage doors. For those staying in a two-story house, go to an interior, first-floor room, the basement, a windowless bathroom, or a closet.

If you are in a multiple-story building and away from the water, go to the first or second floors and take refuge in the halls or other windowless inner rooms. Interior stair wells and the areas around elevator shafts are generally the strongest part of a building. Lie on the floor under tables or other sturdy objects.

If the eye of the hurricane should pass over, be aware that the improved weather conditions are only temporary and that raging storm conditions will soon return with winds coming from the opposite direction.

After the storm passes, stay in the protected area until announcements are made on the radio or television that the dangerous winds have subsided.

After the hurricane has passed or deteriorated, beware of outdoor hazards including downed power lines and the water into which they may have fallen. Beware of weakened bridges and washed-out roads. Watch for weakened limbs on trees, damaged overhanging structures and leaning or broken telephone poles (Figure 8.5). When cutting up

Figure 8.5 A cracked telephone pole re-sembles a large tooth-pick as it precariously leans over Kuhio High-way (Route 56) near Anahola.

fallen trees, use caution, especially if you use a chain saw. Serious injuries can occur when these powerful machines snap back or when the chain breaks.

Do not use the telephone unless absolutely necessary. Guard against spoiled food by using only canned, dried and other nonperishable types of food. Do not drink or prepare food with tap water until you are certain it is not contaminated. Avoid using candles and other open flames indoors.

Recent Hurricanes

Few years have passed without hurricane activity in the ocean waters surrounding Hawaii. In 1993, two Category 4 and one Category 3 hurricanes skirted Hawaii. These included Hurricane Eugene, which passed very near the southern tip of the Big Island, Hurricane Keoni and Hurricane

Figure 8.6 *The Honolulu Advertiser* of Sunday, July 2000 hearlding the approach of a large tropical storm. Maui County sent all government workers home to prepare and most businesses and school were closed. The storm never hit. Image captured by GOES-10 satellite.

Fernanda.

The year of 1994 saw three Category 5 hurricanes (Emelia, Gilma and John) barreling toward the state.

Hurricane seasons in both 1995 and 1996 brought little tropical storm or hurricane activity to Hawaii. This was attributed to La Niña, in which ocean temperatures remain colder.

The major potential threat for 1997 was Hurricane Felicia, a Category 4. Increased cyclonic activity occurred in 1998 and 1999 with Hurricanes Dora, Eugene, Fernanda and Estelle. In 2000, a very severe threat brought Maui and Oahu Civil Defense officials to their knees from July 24 through August 4 as Hurricane Daniel took aim at Maui, but changed course and was downgraded to tropical storm status.

The Next Hurricane

Like a spinning top, hurricanes in Hawaiian waters and in the great Pacific Ocean are capricious and unpredictable. We may find comfort, however, in the fact that we have the means to assess and prepare for these potential disasters.

Hawaii's residents and visitors can be relatively sure that another hurricane will strike one or more of the Hawaiian Islands in the future. It may not hit during this hurricane season or even the next, but Hawaii is certain to face more tempests in the future.

With sophisticated technology, adequate warning will probably be provided. Will islanders comprehend the warning and seriously make long-term plans for the next hurricane? That is up to you.

§§§§§

Chapter Nine

Last Thoughts From the Heart of Kauai

In the aftermath of a severe natural disaster, people had the opportunity to reflect on their experience and what is important in life. Kauai's hurricane victims felt compelled to share their learning experiences in the hopes that others may learn, too.

Donna Goodwin:

"The most important thing I learned from this hurricane was that material things don't matter - not houses, not money, not cars . . . All the things men build can be taken away in the twinkling of an eye. What's really important is the bond between people and between all that we call God, or a Higher Power."

Reverend Harold Kilborn:

"The most important thing I learned from the hurricane is that life shouldn't be taken for granted. I think the hurricane was God's way of giving us a new lease on life, hopefully with a different perspective. We are here today and gone tomorrow. What's important is making our lives count and staying in close relationship with our creator."

Pippa Smith:

"I used to think I didn't need people, that I was fine on

my own. But after the storm, I realized how much we need each other. I felt stripped down. I asked myself, 'Why do we surround ourselves with so many material things?' I think it's to distract us from joining others in intimate relationships. We keep ourselves very busy with worry about our belongings and about passing them on to our children. We lose touch with what really counts, our relation to one another."

Clark Sealy:

"I learned to take one day at a time. That was part of my philosophy before the storm, but during and after it, it was clearer than ever before that, in a matter of moments, your entire life can change."

Iwa Batalona:

"The most important thing I learned from the hurricane was that friendship and relationships with other people are the most important things to me. We don't have anything else. It can all be taken away."

Ed Kanoi:

"We're so dependent on electricity. To be without it was a great lesson for me. I thought a lot about how compli-cated we've made our lives. We work all day and, with the help of electricity and computers, squeeze in more work at night. Nature just came along and said, 'You're going without for a while. Life is going to be very simple. You get up when the sun does, you do whatever work you can, and when the sun goes down, you go home to sleep.' Maybe squeezing every last little bit of energy out of ourselves to keep doing things is not the right way to live."

Irene Anderson:

"I'll always stay on Kauai, despite living through two hurricanes and a tidal wave on this island. To stay on this spot on the earth, our taro patch above Hanalei Bay, I'd live in a tent if I had to. I haven't found people like Kauai people anywhere else. People here care more about others than they do about themselves. You'd see it down at the hurricane shelter when we were passing out supplies, the basic necessities. I'd tell people who , I knew had big families, 'Take more.' They'd reply, 'No. Leave that for somebody else.'"

Landis Ignacio:

"I was born and raised on Kauai and I'll die here. There's no place like Kauai, or Hawaii. I think the hurricane has helped me to be a stronger person. It's made me aware of things and people I took for granted. It made me aware of the fragility of our ecosystem. And it made me realize how dependent people are on one another."

Bill Glasscock:

"Community is real important. I was deeply impressed with my neighbors, all pitching in and working together. We were actually criticized for cleaning up our homes and neighborhood. We would have gotten more government funds if we'd left the mess instead of repairing our roofs. But, we didn't expect anything from the government. We had food, water and shelter, so we were free to go help others."

Keith Robinson:

"I learned that if you build a house strong enough, even if it's simple or a bit ugly, it could stand up to 200 mph winds. You might not even need insurance. If you construct the house

146

right and make a few preparations before hand, you're likely to be all right. You just go back to wood heaters and kerosene lanterns . . . like we had when I was a boy on Niihau.

"I actually kind of liked it after Iniki when there was no power or phone service. The telephone didn't ring, the tax man wasn't after us and the government wasn't harassing us. It was a very peaceful time . . . not all that bad."

Karen Holck:

"I learned how resilient we human beings are. In spite of losing my home and almost losing some of my family, it never entered my mind to leave Kauai. But I'm going to be a smart little piggy this time. I'm going to build a house the winds can't blow down -- a concrete house with a storm cellar."

§§§§§

Figure 9.1 Irene Anderson stands in front of her hurricane-ravaged home in Hanalei following Iniki in 1992.

References

Anderson, Robert N. and Gary R. Vieth, et.al. **Kauai Socioeconomic Profile**. Honolulu: Center for Nonmetropolitan Planning and Development, 1975.

"Bargain Sale of Chickens Ends 20 Year Effort." **The Garden Island.** 12 August 1959. 1:8, 2:3

Blay, Charles and Rob Seimers. **The Geology of Kauai**. Kekaha: TEOK Investigations, 1997.

Burleigh, Betty. "Tourists Took Hurricane in Stride at Shelters". **The Garden Island**. 12 August 1959.

Chandler, Kapeka. Personal interview. December 1993.

Chiu, Arthur N.L. and Luis E. Escalante, et.al. **Hurricane Iwa Experience and Coastal Flood Hazard Estimation in Hawaii.** Honolulu: Environmental Center, University of Hawaii, 1983.

Chiu, Arthur N.L. and Luis E. Escalante, et. al. **Hurricane Iwa, Hawaii November 23, 1982**. Washington, D.C.: National Academy Press, 1983.

Cook, Chris. Journalist. Personal Interview. October 1992.

Cooper, George and Gavan Dawes. **Land and Power in Hawaii.** Honolulu: University of Hawaii Press, 1990

County of Kauai, Department of Planning and Economic Development. **Economic Development on the Island of Kauai: Issues and Options.** Lihue: Kauai Committee, 1985.

Cox, Doak C. **Hurricane Iwa Experience and Coastal Flood Hazard Estimation in Hawaii**. Honolulu : Environmental Center, University of Hawaii, 1983.

Dawes, Gavan. **Shoal of Time: A History of the Hawaiian Islands.** Honolulu: University of Hawaii Press, 1968.

Dionne, Roger. "It's Not Much Fun Being A Hurricane Dot Evacuee." **The Honolulu Advertiser**. 9 August 1959. A:6.

Faye, Michael. Manager, KikiaolaLand Company. Personal Interview, March 1993.

Fujimoto, Richard. Interview. **Honolulu Advertiser**. 3 December 1957.

Gerardo, Sonny. Personal interview, December 1992.

Haraguchi, Paul. **Hurricane Iwa, Circular C91**. Honolulu: State of Hawaii, Department of Land and Natural Resources, 1983.

Haviland, Julie. personal Interview. February, 1993.

Hawaii Visitors Bureau. **Annual Research Report**. Honolulu: HVB, 1960.

Hawaii Visitors Bureau **Yearly visitor statistic reports 1981 - 1993.**

Holck, Karen. Personal Interview. January 1993.

Honolulu Advertiser. September 27, 1959.

Honolulu Star-Bulletin. December 2, 1957.

Hoverson, Margaret, ed. **Historic Koloa: A Guide**. Koloa: Friends of the Koloa Community/School Library, 1985.

H&S Publishing. "INIKI." **Kauai Business Magazine**. Kapaa: H & S Publishing, 1992.

Jarves, James J. "A Trip Through Central America: Being Observations From My Note-Book During the Years 1837-1842." **Scenes and Scenery in the Sandwich Islands**. Boston: James Munroe and Company, 1843.

Joesting, Edward. **Kauai: The Separate Kingdom**. Honolutu: University of Hawaii Press and the Kauai Museum Association, Ltd., 1984.

Kauai Bicentennial Committee. **Waimea: Island of Kauai 1778-1978.** Waimea: Bicentennial Committee, 1977.

Kikuchi, William (Pila). Professor, Kauai Community College. Anthropology Lecture. October, 1998.

Kilborn, Harold. Pastor, Koloa Church. Personal Interview. March 1993.

Kirch, Patrick Vinton. **Feathered Gods and Fishooks: An Introduction to Hawaiian Archaeology and Prehistory**. Honolulu: University of Hawaii Press, 1985.

Kimbro, Betty and Mary Ann Woosley , ed. **Hurricane Iwa Hits Hawaii**. Honolulu: C.F. Boone, 1982.

Kunimura, Phyllis. Personal Interview July 1997.

Kuykendall, R.S. **The Hawaiian Kingdom 1778-1854**. Honolulu: University of Hawaii Press, 1938.

Luomala, Katherine. **Voices on the Wind: Polynesian Myths and Chants**. Honolulu: Bishop Museum Press, 1986

Lyons, Walter A. "Weather Fundamentals". **The Handy Weather Answer Book**. Detroit: Visible Ink, 1997.

Lyons, Walter A . "Hurricanes and Tropical Storms." **The Handy Weather Answer Book**. Detroit: Visible Ink, 1997

Mark, Shelley M. "Emerging Patterns in Hawaiian Business and Industry." **Modern Hawaii: Perspectives on the Hawaiian Community.** Labor Management Education Program, University of Hawaii, Honolulu, 1967.

Nakuina, Moses. **The Wind Gourd of Laomaomao.** Translated by Esther T. Mookini and Sarah Nakoa. Honolulu: Kalamaku Press, 1990

"Nina's Course Tracked by Planes." **The Garden Island**. December 4, 1957. A-1.

Oliver, Dennis. Personal Interview. July 1995.

"Red Cross Forecasts Less Disaster Relief.' **The Garden Island** . August 1959. 1:7

Rosendal, Hans. Lead Forecaster, National Weather Service. Personal interviews and correspondence December 1992 - January 1999.

Schmidt, Robert C. **Historical Statistics of Hawaii**. Honolulu: University Press of Hawaii, 1977.

Schroeder, Thomas. **Hawaiian Hurricanes: Their History, Causes, and the Future**. Technical Document No. 1. Honolulu: University of Hawaii, 1993.

Shaw, Samuel et. al. **A History of Tropical Cyclones in the Central North Pacific & Hawaiian Islands 1832-1979**. Honolulu: U.S. Department of Commerce, National Oceanic and Atmospheric Administration, 1981.

Shoemaker, James H. "Economic Transformations since the War." **Modern Hawaii: Perspectives on the Hawaiian Community.** Labor Management Education Program, University of Hawaii. Honolulu 1967.

Stewart, Donna, ed. **The Kauai Data Book Fifth Edition**. Kapaa: H&S Publishing, 1994.

Takaaki, Ronald. **Pau Hana: Plantation Life and Labor in Hawaii 1835-1920**. Honolulu: University of Hawaii Press, 1983.

Tehada, James. Kauai County Councilman. Personal Interview. June 1995.

U.S. Army Corps of Engineers, Pacific Ocean Division. **Post Disaster Report: Hurricane Iwa 23 November 1982**. Honolulu, 1983.

U.S. Army Corps of Engineers, Pacific Ocean Division, Flood Plain Management Section, Planning Branch. **Hurricane Vulnerability Study for Honolulu, Hawaii and Vicinity, Vol. I Hazard Analysis.** Honolulu: Government Printing Office, 1985.

United States. Department of Agriculture Statistical Reporting Service. "1961-1989 Annual Reports by Hawaii Crop and Livestock Reporting Service." **Statistics of Hawaiian Agriculture.** Honolulu: Hawaii State Department of Agriculture, 1989.

United States. Federal Emergency Management Agency. **Hazard Mitigation Report: Hurricane Iniki** FEMA-961 -DR-H: 1993 .

United States. State of Hawaii. **Statistical and Economic Report.** Honolulu: State Government Publication, 1991.

Yukimura, JoAnn. Former Kauai County Mayor. Personal interview. January 1997.

To order copies of this book, please write to:

Primitive Graffiti
P.O. Box 7.69
Kalaheo, Hawaii.

Fill out the following information and eclose a check or money order for $10.95 and $3.50 for shipping.

Name _____

Address _____

City_____

Zip Code _____

Tales of the Tempests
TheHurricanes of Kauai

§§§§§

To order copies of this book, please write to:

Primitive Graffiti
P.O. Box 7.69
Kalaheo, Hawaii.

Fill out the following information and eclose a check or money order for $10.95 and $3.50 for shipping.

Name _____

Address _____

City_____

Zip Code _____

Tales of the Tempests
TheHurricanes of Kauai

ƧƧƧƧƧ

To order copies of this book, please write to:

Primitive Graffiti
P.O. Box 7.69
Kalaheo, Hawaii.

Fill out the following information and eclose a check or money order for $10.95 and $3.50 for shipping.

Name _____

Address _____

City_____

Zip Code _____

Tales of the Tempests
TheHurricanes of Kauai

$$\text{\textbf{SSSSS}}$$

To order copies of this book, please write to:

Primitive Graffiti
P.O. Box 7.69
Kalaheo, Hawaii.

Fill out the following information and eclose a check or money order for $10.95 and $3.50 for shipping.

Name _____

Address _____

City_____

Zip Code _____

Tales of the Tempests
TheHurricanes of Kauai

ϛϛϛϛϛ

To order copies of this book, please write to:

Primitive Graffiti
P.O. Box 7.69
Kalaheo, Hawaii.

Fill out the following information and eclose a check or money order for $10.95 and $3.50 for shipping.

Name _____

Address _____

City_____

Zip Code _____

Tales of the Tempests
TheHurricanes of Kauai

ççççç